treason

treason

Poems by

HÉDI KADDOUR

Translated from the French by

MARILYN HACKER

Yale University Press • New Haven & London

Published with assistance from the Kingsley Trust Association Publication Fund established by the Scroll and Key Society of Yale College.

This work, published as part of a program providing publication assistance, received financial support from the French Ministry of Foreign Affairs, the Cultural Services of the French Embassy in the United States and FACE (French American Cultural Exchange).

Designed by Mary Valencia. Set in Adobe Garamond type by Tseng Information Systems, Inc. Printed in the United States of America by Sheridan Books, Ann Arbor, Michigan.

Library of Congress Cataloging-in-Publication Data
Kaddour, Hédi.
[Poems. English & French. Selections]
Treason : poems / by Hédi Kaddour ; translated from the French by Marilyn Hacker.
p. cm.
ISBN 978-0-300-14958-6 (alk. paper)
1. Kaddour, Hédi— Translations into English. I. Hacker, Marilyn, 1942– II. Title.
PQ2671.A277A2 2010
841'.914—dc22   2009033260

A catalogue record for this book is available from the British Library.
This paper meets the requirements of ANSI/NISO Z39.48–1992 (Permanence of Paper).
10 9 8 7 6 5 4 3 2 1

contents

PROMENADE EN VILLE :: A WALK IN THE CITY

VARIATIONS :: VARIATIONS

translator's preface

Even in these days of electronic mail and mass transit, I suspect that the writer-flâneur still exists in every city. I know he, sometimes she, still strolls through and observes Paris, the city meant for walkers, where the idea of the ambulant urban spectator originated in the works of Charles Baudelaire, Walter Benjamin, Louis Aragon (the "paysan de Paris"), Raymond Queneau, and Jacques Réda. One of his current incarnations is a slender man in jeans and a black leather jacket, pale, slightly unshaven, with a shock of wavy black hair, a wry smile, listening to an omnipresent Walkman or, these days, occasionally consulting a text on a smartphone. Many of Hédi Kaddour's poems arise from observations, from situations seized *sur le vif,* that might be ordinary but are nonetheless emblematic—of contemporary life, of human stubbornness, human invention, or human cruelty, of the way the past invisibly inflects and inflicts the present.

I first encountered a group of Hédi Kaddour's poems in the summer of 2000, in *Po&sie,* the literary journal founded by the poet and philosopher Michel Deguy: a sequence of fourteen-liners with the general title "Passage au Luxembourg." They were a walker's, a watcher's, and a listener's poems, sonnet-shaped vignettes with a line or two of dialogue that turned the observation and the poem itself into a kind of miniature theater piece. I was at the time writing a sequence of flâneur sonnets myself, located across the river in another arrondissement, and the pleasurable exercise of translating these poems by a writer hitherto unknown to me (about whom the contributor's note told me little but that there were two books of his poems I might read) seemed like an extension of the work, or the walk, already in progress. It turned out that the poet and translator Claire Malroux, with whom I had worked in both directions, knew Hédi Kaddour from the circle around the journal. I wrote to him, and in response Claire and I were both invited by the poet and his wife to dinner and a short piano recital by their music-conservatory-student daughter on the boulevard du Port-Royal. This was the beginning of a conversation—about poetry, politics, history, the novel, language, memory—that has gone on intermittently until today, over the time in which I did the translations in this book. Much of what I write here about the poet and his work is the fruit of such conversation.

Hédi Kaddour was born in Tunis in 1945 to a Tunisian father and a French Algerian pied-noir mother. He has lived in France since the age of eight, and French is his mother tongue. His view of poetry, though, is that of a comparatist—of a reader owing no allegiance to a single language or a single poetics: the poetries of several languages and literary traditions are lively and constant presences in his mind and in his work. He describes the occasion of writing his first poem: while a teacher of French in Morocco, in the dull stretch of time spent proctoring a long exam, he was reading a poem by Georg Trakl in a German/French bilingual edition. Dissatisfied with the translation, be began to retranslate parts of the text himself; then followed his own lines, rather than the German original, until he had, almost to his surprise, a poem of his own.

Some of the picaresque unpredictability in the life and point of view of this writer are contained in the anecdote. German is his second language, learned at school and pursued at university. Friedrich Hölderlin, Heinrich Heine, Rainer Maria Rilke, and Trakl figure in his poetic pantheon alongside Baudelaire, Guillaume Apollinaire, Jules Supervielle, Stéphane Mallarmé, and the contemporaries Philippe Jaccottet, Yves Bonnefoy, André du Bouchet, Jacques Réda, and Deguy. Apollinaire himself knew German well. Kaddour notes that in the "Rhénanes," Apollinaire's deliberate insertion of Germanisms in syntax or idiom, directly translated into French, creates an atmosphere of alterity. He has occasionally adopted this technique of assimilated translation into his own work, often in less predictable contexts, steering a poem that begins anecdotally into the less certain and less known.

Kaddour did his French military service in Morocco, in part because of the possibility of joining a fencing team. He used the opportunity to master both literary and dialectal Arabic and embark on the reading of that literature, finally adding an additional university degree in Arabic to those he already had in French literature. He stayed on in Morocco with his wife and daughters for a dozen years as a teacher of French. He has mentioned in conversation that part of his apprenticeship in Arabic consisted of listening to tapes made for him by friends of classical and contemporary poetry and fiction in that language, even before he could fully understand the texts. This oral reception of text and tongue remains important to him regardless of the language in question: recorded books in English or German (in which he is not yet completely fluent) often accompany him these days on his walks through the city.

Upon returning to France in the late 1980s, he worked as a journalist for the magazines *L'Autre Journal* and *Politis* for four years and then continued writing music and theater criticism for the *Nouvelle revue française* while pursuing a teaching career at the Ecole normale supérieure. He also undertook translations of contemporary German poets including Ingeborg Bachmann and Durs Grünbein, and has prefaced the work of Hans Magnus Enzensberger for the paperback classic Poésie Gallimard series. He began publishing his own poetry in the 1980s, first with small presses, Obsidiane and Ipomée, and later with Gallimard. He is also an expert in European classical music (the aforementioned daughter is now an emerging concert pianist), and a bemused /amused scholar and observer of modern and contemporary history, with a particular interest in the events surrounding and subsequent to World War I. After years in the fifth arrondissement, he presently lives in one of Paris's near suburbs—still an easy walk into the city center. He is a frequent contributor to the *Nouvelle revue française* and a member of the editorial committee of *Po&sie*. Kaddour's journalist's skills and instinct for observation, for seizure of the salient detail, are put to work in his poems, as is the invaluable ability to become a "significant absence"—not a Rimbaldian absconder but an observer who eschews inference—from many of his own texts. He also cites the theater critic's skill of capturing in a few concise sentences something of the narrative, the direction, the physical presence, the actors' interpretation of a play as something that has served, indeed helped to shape his own goals as a poet. The dramatist and the reporter are both at work in many poems here, as in the opening of "The Question":

> *Do you work for the dough or to*
> *Get laid,* the nurse is asked by
> A woman who's brought in by the police.

Kaddour's work combines an often surprising sensuality with erudition and wit, while it questions the structures of syntax itself and the limits of poetic form. Along with his friend and contemporary Guy Goffette, he is one of the few current French poets whose work one could place in a direct line from that of Réda and Jacques Roubaud—but where the horizons of Réda's poems tend to be local, Kaddour's vary. There is a strain of his poetic work that is as local and specific to his urban residence as are the Paris poems of Baudelaire, Apollinaire, Jacques Prévert, or Queneau. An observed singular occurrence, a coincidence, a situation at once natural and unexpected, will be the starting point of one of his compressed narratives:

> What has gotten into the bus driver
> Who has left his bus, who has sat down
> On a curb on the place de l'Opéra? ["The Bus Driver"]

Walking along the river, purchasing a pastry in a bakery, a few words exchanged with a bookseller, waiting in line at a concert hall may provide Kaddour with the start of a poem: notes taken on the spot, never a solitary meditation over a blank piece of paper. Other poems, however, have the breadth, even in condensed forms, of the work of Derek Walcott and Louis MacNeice. These sometimes focus on the intersections of French and North African history, sometimes on the tortuous evolution of Europe after World War I:

> But Arabs, you know
> what hotheads they are . . . Her husband shut her up, left first,
> came back plus a medal, less a leg, a list
> of all the Mohammeds dead at Verdun. She exclaimed, *"It's
> madness, not you, there in Russia . . ."* ["Poppies"]

Many poems evoke other poets whose work is a continual reference point for the writer, with a technique not dissimilar to that of Guy Goffette's *"Dilectures,"* engaging at once with the other's text and persona. A phrase, an image, or an anecdote gives rise to a concise portrait, a dialogue with more than a homage to Jorge Luis Borges, Paul Celan, Joseph Brodsky, the politically engaged Czech poet Vladimir Holan, the French minimalist Jean Follain, or the trilingual Alsatian Jean-Paul de Dadelsen.

> he's put *white tulips*
>
> Instead of *black firs:* Paul
>
> Celan didn't like tall trees. You
>
> Never knew him, and you like these poems?

a bookseller asks the narrator in "Quai des Orfèvres."

As these names imply, Kaddour's references range from the undisputed figures of "world" poetry, translated into every language, to somewhat marginalized, nonmainstream (and rarely translated) French poets.

Still, most of the poetic encounters that Kaddour describes as crucial to his own formation as a writer are with European writers of other than French language and history, and often with the experience of displacement or exile. One of his signal discoveries in the late 1980s was Brodsky's essay collection *Far from Byzantium* (in the French translation of Laurence Dyère and Véronique Schilz), which he read along with Brodsky's poetry: essays which are meditations on history as well as on the work of individual poets: Anna Akhmatova, Osip Mandelstam, Marina Tsvetaeva, but also C. P. Cavafy, W. H. Auden, and Walcott. His presentation of Brodsky in an essay of his own in the *Nouvelle revue française* in 1989 constituted the serious introduction of the Russian émigré poet to a French readership. Kaddour found in Brodsky something of a kindred spirit: a writer who had endured history's horrors and vagaries but (or therefore) remained skeptical and independent of political and aesthetic pieties, steeped in the classical traditions of his own and other literatures while open to an absolute contemporaneity.

> But one day he emptied his closets
>
> Of suits which would have been all too

Becoming to the enemy, and he went off
Toward a wind from beyond those lands.

> —from "A Victim's Soul," Kaddour's poem-homage to Brodsky

Literature, for Hédi Kaddour, whether it be poetry or fiction, is also the past of literature—the poetry of today contains the poetry of the past. Writing cannot be all memory, or it would satisfy itself with repeating the past, which would produce, at best, mass-market literature. But neither can it eliminate memory totally: in that case, it condemns itself to be disposed of in its turn. That, he says is the meaning of Supervielle's reference to "oublieuse mémoire"—*forgetful memory:* forgetfulness in order not to repeat what was previously done, memory so as not to succumb to amnesia. Kaddour shares with Brodsky too an obliquity of approach: the life of the polis is present in his poems, injustice and violence as well, but seen from an angle, and never editorialized upon.

Kaddour's poetry often converses with classical forms, the sonnet in particular, though he uses the fourteen-line poem in a way that might remind American readers of Robert Lowell's quatorzains, especially of the volume called *History* in its collaging of public and private events and its urban portraits. Kaddour's collection *Passage au Luxembourg* is, except for one poem, made up entirely of a hundred-odd quatorzains, many of which are in this present book. It contains a sequence congruent with the title, another based on scenes from Breughel that are more portraits of carnal human nature than ekphrastic poems. Other poems achieve (as sonnets can) a delicate and witty balance between eroticism and a certain misanthropy, which is not at all misogyny. Even the erotic poems maintain a delicate balance in locating the speaker: either a narrator or a participant in the act might describe the woman in "High Cheekbones":

She was the first
To kiss and is still surprising herself
With her own sweetness as she watches her leg
Rise toward the antique chandelier.

Kaddour has played with the formal aspect in successive versions of these poems, initially using the classical structure of two quatrains and two tercets, then closing up the poems into a single block, sometimes drastically shortening the lines. In English we are more used to identifying as sonnets poems which are not broken into four quatrains and two tercets. French poetic nomenclature has resisted this, leading in part to a paucity of discussion of the contemporary French sonnet and a near-assumption of its demise, while a foreign reader would see its continuation in Roubaud, certainly, but also in Kaddour and Goffette.

Kaddour makes a surprisingly sharp differentiation between his own urban "sonnets" and Baudelaire's. In Baudelaire and, I would add, in Verlaine, and in the work of Goffette as well, a subjectivity inherited from the Romantics is almost persistently present, whereas in Kaddour's poems, it is more frequently absent except in the persona of a bemused and not at all omniscient observer: a trait shared with Apollinaire's "Rhénanes" or the short poems of Follain (these latter resemblances pointed out by Kaddour himself). The absent "I" is not uncommon in contemporary French poetry, but the insistent, lively presence of a quotidian specific not overshadowed by subjectivity sets Kaddour's poetry somewhat apart. If he resembles the Lowell of *History,* the "confessional" aspect of *The Dolphin* is entirely foreign to his project, while the narrative arc fragmented into salient anecdotes in independent poems which could also be viewed as stanzaic, found in (for example) Hayden Carruth or contemporaries like George Szirtes, Alfred Corn, or Derek Mahon, is more familiar to it. These correspondences are my own interjections. Kaddour's frame of reference in contemporary poetry is not predominantly Anglophone—his touchstones in American poetry are William Carlos Williams and Wallace Stevens—unless the exiled Brodsky can also be considered an American poet.

The poems in this collection are taken from three books published by Gallimard: *La fin des vendanges* (The End of the Wine Harvest, 1989); *Jamais une ombre simple* (Never a Simple Shadow, 1994), and *Passage au Luxembourg* (2000). Following the poet's arrangement of his own books, I have taken the liberty of arranging them more thematically than chronologically: poems to do with history and with precursors; poems that cross Paris on foot; poems to do with erotic and familial relations; and poems to do with music, which is always close to the intimate for this poet. Kaddour's first novel, *Waltenberg,* was published by Gallimard in 2005 and received the Prix Goncourt du premier roman: an English translation has been published in Great Britain by Harvill Secker. (One day, he says, he came home from a stroll in the city with notes for a poem; developing them, he realized that he was going to write a long novel instead, though some of the themes of the novel had already been addressed in a play written in the 1990s.) He is at present completing a second novel, in tandem with a nonfiction prose narrative that combines acute informal literary criticism with the kind of witty, honed, fine observation of quotidian life in Paris that I find in his poems (both to be published in 2010 by Gallimard). And first drafts of their chapters were also composed while walking across the pont d'Austerlitz from the thirteenth arrondisement to the quai de la Rapée or alongside the sailboat pond in the Luxembourg Gardens on a foggy October afternoon.

LOIN DE BYZANCE :: FAR FROM BYZANTIUM

Le troupeau

Portes ouvertes à l'espacement
De la colline où se déploient
La poudre du matin, la métaphore
De beige et bleu, les tintements
Comme réponse au grand cortège
Des nuages à cul plat : la canne,
Un groupe et son berger s'en vont
Au pas qui mène hors de portée
Vers un temps qui se gagne, et jusque
Dans l'œil des lièvres la vérité
Vient guetter alentour. Approche,
Rien n'empêche, on en serait jaloux,
On oublierait l'idée qu'un mouton
Meurt rarement de vieillesse.

The Flock

Doors flung open on the hillside's
Outspread space where there are, unfurled,
The powder of morning, the metaphor
Of beige and blue, a tinkling
Like a response to the grand cortege
Of flat-bottomed clouds: the staff,
A flock, and its shepherd go off
At a pace which leads them out of sight
Toward a time which is earned, and even
In hares' eyes the truth
Draws near, lies in wait around them. Come closer,
Nothing's stopping you, you could envy them,
Forgetting the fact that a sheep
Rarely dies of old age.

Arbres

La milice qui croyait tellement
Aux grands chênes
Qu'elle les garnissait de pendus.

Celui qui contemple les arbres
A parfois la froideur
Du renard guettant les corbeaux
Jusqu'à ce qu'il lui en tombe un,
Sur la gueule, gelé.

Trees

The militia which had such faith
In tall oaks
That it festooned them with hanged men.

He who gazes at trees
Sometimes has the cold indifference
Of a fox who stares at the crows
Until one drops to him
Right on his snout, frozen.

Noces du chacal

Quand le ciel restait trop longtemps
bleu intense, il arrivait que les gens
se vêtissent de gris et de terne.
Comme en appel. Parfois même,
un peu de pluie pouvait tomber.
Alors — entre la terre rousse des collines,
le plomb volatile du crachin
et les premiers brins de l'orge
— il y avait comme un éclair du soleil
et l'arc-en-ciel surgissait.
Cela s'appelait les noces du chacal.

The Jackal's Wedding

When the sky had stayed too intensely
blue for too long, it sometimes happened that people
dressed in gray and in dull colors.
Like an appeal. Sometimes a little
rain would even fall.
Then—between the red earth of the hills
the volatile lead of the drizzle,
and the first shoots of barley
—there was a kind of sunlight flash
and the rainbow sprang forth.
This was called the jackal's wedding.

La détresse spirituelle

Et marre des faiseurs d'almanachs qui vous
laissent pris entre les dettes, la mort,
ou la semaine des sept demains. Aujourd'hui
c'est encore un monsieur : « *Les convulsions
de l'histoire, monstrueuse métaphore de notre
détresse spirituelle.* » Regarde donc, détresse :
Burgos, au Moyen âge, un fils de boulanger
se convertit au christianisme, et le père entre
en telle fureur qu'il le jette dans le four.
Sainte Marie, dit la chronique, sauva le fils,
les habitants de Burgos brûlèrent le père et

ne t'éloigne pas trop, détresse, vers le fou rire,
car la suite est une énigme : mon premier
est un convoi de juifs envoyés à Auschwitz par
la Préfecture de Gironde; mon second, un cortège
d'Algériens noyés par balles qui défilent
sous le pont Mirabeau; mon troisième le trésor
d'un grand parti national dans les années soixante,
mon tout doit être *le nom propre* d'une grande
détresse spirituelle et ne s'appelle surtout pas
Martin Heidegger et ne vous énervez pas, l'énervant
c'est que tout ça ne soit plus qu'allusion.

Spiritual Distress

And damn the almanac makers who leave you
stuck between debts and death
or a week with seven tomorrows. Today
here's another gent: *History's convulsions,*
monstrous metaphor of our
spiritual distress. Listen to this, distress:
in Burgos, in the Middle Ages, a baker's son
converted to Christianity, and his father,
in a fury, flung him into the oven.
Saint Mary, says the chronicle, saved the son, and
the citizens of Burgos burned the father and

don't wander too far off, distress, and start to giggle
because what comes next is a riddle: my first is
a convoy of Jews sent to Auschwitz by
the Préfecture of the Gironde; my second, a procession
of bullet-bloated Algerians who float
under the pont Mirabeau; my third the funding
of the party in power in the sixties,
and together they make the *proper name* of a great
spiritual distress which is certainly not called
Martin Heidegger and don't get annoyed, what's annoying
is that all this should merely be allusion.

Trahison

« Les poètes n'ont pas la pudeur de leurs aventures : ils les exploitent. »
—F. NIETZSCHE

Qu'ils n'aient rien à se mettre dans la bouche
pour le dernier voyage! Des mois entiers de courses
au grand marché — pas drôle du tout, si, des fois,
quand le soleil embrase le cœur du monde
et qu'on que la voix se précipite pour empêcher
que ça vous saute aux yeux c'est maladroit
comme le cycle inquiet des endocrines
alors on se met à trois ou quatre derrière
une grasse matrone, le taffetas collé à la peau
par des inondations de sueur et on lui gueule
en pleine allée centrale *madame, madame, le cul
y mange la robe !* Et file entre les cageots, tandis
que rouge, vert, ocre, l'espace rebalance
les grandes claques de son rire. Halte au cœur :
avec dix francs de longue épargne on l'avait,
le ballon *made in France* avec odeur de cuir
et penalties presque à neuf mètres, grands matchs,
grands cris, grandes bagarres jusqu'à la nuit
du temps qui ne dormira pas, quand les hautes
chandelles rendent aux étoiles un peu de l'énergie
qui nous en vient, avec dix francs, le con
d'leur mère à ces tarés du testicule, ils avaient
filé droit chez une putain à forte touffe.

Treason

"Poets lack modesty in their adventures: they exploit them."
—F. NIETZSCHE

May they have nothing to fill their mouths
on their last journey! Months of running errands
in the marketplace—no fun at all, but sometimes,
when the sun sets the heart of the world on fire
and your voice rushes up to stop
everyone seeing it, it's as awkward
as your uneasy hormone surges,
so three or four of you gang up behind
a hefty matron, shiny cloth glued to her skin
by floods of sweat, and you shout at her
between the vegetable stalls, *lady, lady, your dress
is up your ass,* and take off around the fruit crates! While
red, green, ocher, the air swings her huge
peals of laughter back at you. Heartstopping:
with ten hard-saved francs you could have
the soccer ball *Made in France* smelling of leather
and penalties at nearly nine yards, great games,
great shouts, great fights until the night
of time which won't sleep, when the tall
candles give back to the stars some of the
energy we get from them, with the ten francs,
those pus-balled motherfuckers, they
went straight to some hairy-cunt whore.

Les coquelicots

Et c'est peut-être vrai que le destin
avait commencé par agioter entre les cascades
et les grands arbres qui sont l'orgueil là-bas
du regard des maîtres quand ils consentent
à délaisser le cul des cousines appauvries.
Qui sait la vérité ? Celui qui a frappé
et celui qui a reçu les coups. Etait venue
d'un Oberland à silences pas très propres
et vivait avec eux, disait *l'eau doit bouillir,*
et *les femmes ont de nouvelles responsabilités,*
aimait aussi dans l'herbe remercier le Dieu
du soleil et des spasmes vaginaux, et quand
on a mis le feu à tous les coquelicots d'Europe,
elle a crié *Les peuples ! Et à Kiental, chez moi,*
les socialistes ! Mais, les arabes, vous savez,
le baroud... son mari la fit taire, partit premier,
revint avec la croix, la jambe en moins, liste
de Mohammed morts à Verdun. Elle criait *C'est*
de la folie, pas vous, il y a là-bas en Russie...
elle trimbalait son estropié, ça l'avait rendue
folle, oui, pas « d'intelligence avec l'ennemi »,
il faut savoir, même pour vingt ans, soigner
les femmes de héros, a dit le procureur.

Poppies

Fate, perhaps it's true that it began
by trading on the futures of waterfalls
and tall trees, the pride there
on the masters' faces when they deign
to spare the asses of their threadbare female cousins.
Who knows the truth? The one who struck the blows
and the one who was beaten. She came
from an Oberland of soiled silences
and lived with them, said, *Water must boil,*
and *Women now have new responsibilities;*
also loved, stretched in the grass, to thank the God
of sunlight and vaginal spasms, and when
they had set fire to all the poppies of Europe
she cried out, *The people! And in my land, in Kiental,*
the socialists! But Arabs, you know
what hotheads they are . . . Her husband shut her up, left first,
came back plus a medal, less a leg, a list
of all the Mohammeds dead at Verdun. She exclaimed, *It's*
madness, not you, there in Russia . . .
she hauled her cripple around, it drove her mad,
yes. Not "dealings with the enemy,"
you must be able, even for twenty years
to take care of heroes' wives, said the prosecutor.

Le moulin

Je suis le point unique, la leçon
D'un paysage où se joignent, le soir,
Rivière, église et vieux moulin :
Le clocher monte, l'arbre tient,
La roue travaille, et l'eau grise
S'en va sous le vent d'hiver,
Laissant passer, entre chaque aube,
De quoi moudre le grain, scier
Les planches des cercueils, et faire
Rêver l'oisif, dans ce roulement calme
Qui continue à fabriquer de l'énergie
Avec le temps qui reste à la matière
Quand les hommes ont fini de crier
Sur le manteau doux de la neige.

The Mill

I am the single point, the lesson
In a landscape where evening links
A stream, a church, and an old mill:
The bell tower rises, the tree stands fast,
The wheel works, and gray water
Flows away beneath the winter wind,
Letting enough pass, from dawn to dawn
To grind grain, to saw
Coffin planks, to make
Idle men dream, in this calm rumbling
Which keeps on fabricating energy
In the time that's left for matter
When mankind has done shouting
Over the soft cloak of snow.

Les fileuses

Celle qui malgré l'hiver a gardé
Aux joues le souvenir des raisins
Suit de l'œil un couple lent ;
Il franchit le pont de pierre
Vers le bout de forêt où s'embusque
L'ombre bleue des renards. Tout cela
Prend silencieusement sa part de haine,
A l'heure où les jeunes femmes
Quittent la maison lourde de neige,
La tête dans la nuit, étourdies d'avoir
Bu du vin en flammes et filé le lin
De leurs draps entre les jeux, les gages
Et les mensonges, sous le regard
Des hommes qui graissaient des courroies.

The Spinners

The one who has kept, in spite of winter
A memory of grapes on her cheeks
Follows a slow couple with her eyes;
They cross the stone bridge toward
A bit of forest where the blue shadows
Of foxes lie in ambush. All that
Silently claims its portion of hate,
At the hour when young women
Leave the house, heavy with snow,
Their heads still full of night, careless from having
Drunk mulled wine and spun
The linen of their sheets between games, forfeits,
And lies, beneath the gaze
Of men waxing harnesses.

La gardeuse d'oies

Je suis la dernière gardeuse d'oies,
Déjà mon propre souvenir, et la baguette
Est là pour affirmer mes intentions :
Je serai grande, j'habiterai la ville,
J'apprendrai que Circée la déesse
Tient elle aussi la férule
Sur des gravures du siècle monarchique
Devant un homme au sexe doux, et mon mari
Sera docile ; j'aurai des fils, ils seront
Médecins, viendront me voir, la peur
Des nuits sera partie, je ne craindrai
Que pour les miens, j'aurai le temps,
Regretterai parfois de n'avoir pas
Rêvé plus fort la forme de ma vie.

The Goose Girl

I am the last goose girl,
Already a memory of myself, and my staff
Is there to affirm my intentions.
I will be someone, I'll live in the city;
I'll learn that the goddess Circe
Holds the rod too
In engravings from a royal century
Before a suave-sexed man, and my husband
Will be docile; I will have sons, they will be
Doctors, will come to see me, the midnight
Terrors will be gone, I will only
Fear for my family, I'll have the time,
Will sometimes regret that I didn't
Dream my life's form more forcefully.

Le serpent

Il y a toujours quelqu'un pour se souvenir
D'une tranche de pastèque mangée à deux
Quand la lumière est à pic
Sur les fontaines à Florence.
Du fond d'un chagrin sans égal on peut
Alors tenir en respect le Vieillard Temps
Et sa manie de tout racler contre les murs ;
Mais lui, avec un savoir-faire plus précis
Que toutes les insomnies, chope la carte postale,
Pisse dessus, et entre deux rires :
« Crétin, ça un événement ? Tu n'es même pas
Capable de te rejoindre, tu as livré
Ton cul aux mouches et tu te plains
De la destinée ! Tout le monde a, comme moi,
D'abord été ce jeune homme qui passe,
En équilibre sur la roue, avec la réussite
Pour l'an qui vient ; la suite,
C'est ce qu'on perd entre les jours et l'ombre,
A trop tailler le buisson des voyelles,
Et c'est toujours trop tard ;
Tu fais le fier parce que tu crois encore
Au vieux chant des noms propres,
Mais tu vaux moins que tes songes
Et seul l'oubli t'aurait permis
De ne pas finir comme le serpent
Qui m'accompagne et qui depuis des siècles
N'en finit pas de se mordre la queue ».

The Serpent

There's always someone to remember
A slice of watermelon you two shared
When the light came straight down
On the fountains of Florence.
From the depths of a matchless grief you can
Then affront Father Time and his obsession
With scraping everything against the walls;
But he, with a know-how more precise
Than all your insomnias, swipes the postcard,
Pisses on it, and between two snickers:
"Idiot, that was an event? You can't even
Agree with yourself, you've sold
Your ass to the flies, and you complain
About fate! Everyone has, even I,
Been that young man who goes by
Balancing on a wheel, with good luck
For the year to come; what follows
Is what's lost between the days and shadows,
Wasting your time pruning the vowel bushes,
And it's always too late;
You put on airs because you still believe
In the old song of proper names,
But you're worth less than your own daydreams
And only forgetfulness would have allowed you
Not to end up like the serpent
Who keeps me company and who for centuries
Hasn't stopped biting his own tail."

La fin des vendanges

Paul Celan

Et tant de choses qui reviennent finir
dans la mare de ce vieil impubère de Narcisse,
parfois même les chants de victimes. A noter
que n'en réchappent pas mieux ceux qui
mordent la première neige, ou se contentent
de serrer bien fort un adjectif. Au fond
personne. Un vrai témoin, serait-ce, dans le vignoble
en étages de pierres roses, la dernière fanfare,
faite avec les débris des autres ? Elle joue, un peu
par la force des choses, tous les répertoires : *plus près
de toi, la jeune garde* et *zim boum boum*. C'est
la fin des vendanges, un an avant retour
de la pourriture noble. La vigne au moins
sait se tendre des pièges, et la poésie. Alors
ne riez pas quand le pendu étrangle sa corde.

The End of the Wine Harvest

Paul Celan

And so many things which return end up
in the swamp of that aged adolescent Narcissus,
sometimes even victims' songs. It should be noted
that those who bite into the first snowfall, or who are
content to passionately hug an adjective,
are not exempted. Finally,
no one. Might that be an authentic witness, in the vineyard
terraced with rosy stones, that last brass band
made of the other ones' debris? It plays a bit
by force of circumstances, of the whole repertory: *nearer
my God to thee, the workers' vanguard* and *tra la la*. It's
the end of the wine harvest, a year before
the noble rot returns. Grapevines at least
know how to set traps for themselves, poetry too. So
don't laugh when the hanged man strangles his own rope.

Jean-Paul de Dadelsen

Cette lumière, soudain, pour allumer le vol
Instable des hirondelles, les bulles
De la carpe, le corps des femmes :
Malgré l'horloge à gros derrière, les mots
Ne devrait mesurer que les heures
Les plus neuves, mais comment se mettre
A l'abri de son propre refrain ? Il fallait
Le savoir, hein, même quand la rime
A cessé d'être raison, à tordre
Les octaves entre les orgues,
La progression fondamentale de la basse,
La route indispensable et puis la villanelle,
Le *tien* qui ne vaut rien mais fait sortir
Deux loups du bois, la dissonante
Mention des couilles : le tout
Dans la kermesse et le temps saugrenu
Et la tunique sans couture, sans mentir.
Je serai nettoyé, disait-il, *si j'éclate*
Au vent comme citrouille vieille. Un peu
De nuit s'y ajoutait pour le cancer
Et la décompression, pour l'accord
Enfin sans mémoire. Il y aura toujours
De quoi remplir un rêve et mettre de l'humain
Dans la matière sonore, mais la musique,
Comme les enfants, c'est toujours
Vers la séparation qu'elle grandit.

Jean-Paul de Dadelsen

That light, all at once, to spark the unsteady
Flight of swallows, the carp's
Bubbles, women's bodies.
Despite the big-assed clock, words
Should only measure the newest
Hours, but how to shelter yourself
From your own refrain? You had
To know, didn't you, even when rhyme
Ceased to be reason, twisting
The octaves between the organs,
The fundamental progression of the bass,
The indispensable journey, and then the villanelle,
The worthless *bird in the hand* which still brings
Two wolves out of the woods, the dissonant
Reference to your balls: all of it
In the county fair and the bizarre weather
And the seamless tunic, honestly.
I would be cleansed, he said, *if I burst
In the wind like an old pumpkin.* A bit
Of night added on for cancer
And decompression, for the chord
At last free of memory. There will always be
Enough to fill a dream and put something human
Into the acoustics, but music
Like children, is always
Growing toward a separation.

L'or des tigres

Jorge Luis Borges

Nous, quand nous renversons le café, nous disons
que c'est par maladresse et que cela porte
bonheur, tant nous voulons que le regard
reste le gouffre de nos hésitations. Mais,
pas de lumière ! sans le noir, l'œil
n'aurait pas de lumière : *Où sont les micros ?*
avait-il commencé, devant son verre, sa canne
et la sirène des pompiers, rue des Ecoles. Puis,
très vite : *le mot moon a été traversé*
par Shakespeare. Il butait contre
ses propres paroles, mais ce qui suivait
s'était longtemps battu sur tous les continents
contre les heures où les poèmes s'en vont
comme des casseroles, par le cul, *le malheur,*
disait-il, *est plus riche que la victoire,*
et *je supprime l'étonnant.* Voici :
une après-midi s'éleva la voix d'un vieil
aveugle, il parlait de la mémoire à des voyeurs
amnésiques et jetait des pièces d'or à la mer.

Tigers' Gold

Jorge Luis Borges

As for us, when we spill our coffee, we say
that we were clumsy and that it brings
good luck, we so much want our gaze
to be the pit in which our doubts hurl themselves. But
no light! Without blackness, the eye
would have no light. *Where are the microphones?*
he began, his glass, his cane in front of him
and the firemen's sirens in the rue des Ecoles. Then,
very quickly: *The word "moon" has been walked upon
by Shakespeare.* He stumbled over
his own words, but what followed
had battled for a long time on every continent
against the hours when poems rust
like saucepans, bottom first. *Misfortune,*
he said, *is more fruitful than victory,*
and *I delete the astonishing.* Here:
one afternoon an old blind man's voice
rose up; he spoke of memory to amnesiac
voyeurs and threw gold pieces in the sea.

A Jean Follain

Cabane à voyager, postée au bord du monde
Nécessaire ; on en part pour d'étranges contrées
Et certains n'en reviendront pas, maîtres
Enfin du temps grondeur et des règles du jeu,

Le regard en allé derrière la musaraigne,
La pie voleuse ou le grand luxe des images
Qu'on fait soi-même ; d'autres, gravement
Estropiés par des pirates devront mentir

Pour expliquer la blessure au genou que mord
L'alcool du pharmacien. Au soir, la nuit
Complice des gardiens détruit l'immense cheminée

Où l'on faisait rôtir sangliers et petits beurres
Tandis que la cabane s'en va dans l'air bleuté
Offrir aux rêveurs ses branches qui fulgurent.

To Jean Follain

A cabin for traveling, stationed at the edge of
The necessary world; point of departure for strange lands
And some never return, masters at last
Of nagging time, and the rules of the game,

Their gaze gone off after the vole,
The magpie, or the luxury of self-made
Images; others, gravely
Wounded by pirates, will have to lie

When they explain that scraped knee still stinging from
The druggist's alcohol. At dusk, the guardians'
Complicit night dismantles the huge fireplace

Where you grilled wild boar and butter cookies
While the cabin flies away in blue-tinged air
To offer dreamers its flashing branches.

Les petites infamies

Il y eut d'abord ceux qui cherchaient
les enterrements pour s'y gifler à satiété puis
vinrent les prophètes mais quand on les aime encore
ceux-là, c'est seulement pour leurs figures,
la parataxe et zim, la fracassante : la poésie
se souvient, c'est le dernier moulin qui puisse
moudre avec de l'eau déjà partie, des mots
qu'on garde au tourniquet, un tour pour la défaite,
un tour au Prince de Ligne : *Elle est entrée*
— Qui ça ? — La mort ma poule ! et musique
pour les rêves, leurs volutes, mais vous savez
un jour on en finit

                même avec la fumée des cigarettes :
restent leurs sœurs quotidiennes, les petites
infamies, on les garde, on les sert aux grandes
âmes ne pleurez pas *les pleureuses,* monsieur,
ne sont jamais là que pour voler le sexe du mort,
et quand ça proteste on fait comme on fait
aux menteurs, on raccompagne jusqu'à la porte,
on veut entrer pour vérifier, on les menace
de la belle histoire du naturothérapeute
(diplôme canadien) qui plongeait la tête
des adolescents dans la cuvette des wc
pour les calmer sans mouiller leurs vêtements.

The Little Disgraces

First there were those who sought out funerals
to slap themselves to their hearts' content, then came
the prophets, but when you still care for them,
that lot, it's only for their rhetoric,
parataxis and zim, its staggering: poetry
remembers, it's the last mill which might
grind with water that's already flowed away, words
you line up at a turnstile: turn once for the defeat,
turn once for Prince de Ligne: *She's arrived*
— Who's that? — Death, babe! And music
for dreams, their scrolls and coils, but one day
you're done with them,
                          even with cigarette smoke:
their daily sisters remain, the little
disgraces, you keep them, you serve them up
to great spirits, no mourning, *hired mourners,* sir,
are only there to steal the dead man's sex,
and when the great spirits protest you do
what one does with liars, you accompany them
to their front door, you want to go in to check, you threaten them
with the story of the naturotherapist
(Canadian diploma) who thrust the heads
of adolescents into toilet bowls
to calm them down without wetting their clothes.

Récréation

Tu lis Jean-Claude Renard, ou Kenneth White
la plume à la main, car aujourd'hui
Hölderlin ou Montaigne te font peur ; tu appelles cela
piller les zozos, mais de peu, car c'est vraiment
trop mou, même le soleil, comme chez ceux
qui pour garder leurs femmes les enlaidissent. Alors
l'inspiration, bien sûr ; mais pourquoi faut-il
qu'elle n'apparaisse jamais qu'à l'heure du repas
ou de la sieste ?
                  Il vaut mieux se confier
à la promenade en compagnie de Philarion, *drathaar*
parfaitement désobéissant
                        et rouleur de caniches
dans les débris de coquillages venus du temps
infatigable ; et te voilà comme un flûtiste en exercice
de respiration continue, devant les cormorans,
les pétrels, et les couples de retraités du bord de mer
qui ramassent doucement fin octobre le bois mort
des plages, tout cela dans les transparents échanges
des silicates et du lointain : c'est le vent nocturne
de la terre qui a rendu l'air si vif, et si claires
les libellules copulant en plein vol comme des forcenées
de la grande lumière ; et quand tu as relevé les yeux
pour voir ce qu'en pensait la promeneuse
aux seins nus, elle était déjà dix mètres derrière toi.

Recess

You read Jean-Claude Renard or Kenneth White
pen in hand, because today
Hölderlin or Montaigne scare you; you call this
looting the nitwits, but not of much, because
it's really too lame, even the sun, like those men
who, to keep their wives faithful, make them ugly. Then
there's inspiration of course, but why must it
always come only at mealtimes
or during a nap?
                 Better to go for a walk
accompanied by Philarion, perfectly
disobedient *drathaar,*
                      and poodle humper
in the shell debris washed up from tireless
time; and there you are like a flautist
doing endless breathing exercises in front of the cormorants
and petrels and the retired seaside couples
who at the end of October mildly collect driftwood
on the beach, all that in the limpid exchange
of silicates and distance: it's the earth's
night wind that's made the air so brisk and made
the fireflies so bright, copulating in flight like
fresh-air fanatics; and when you raised your eyes to see
what the bare-breasted stroller thought of all this
she was already ten yards behind you.

Septembre

La lampe noire à la hanche de l'aube,
combien de temps va-t-elle tenir
avec son déjà vu dans la rêverie des mots
à contre-jour ? Il y a tant d'autres choses
tout aussi graves, et plus précises : la ligne
où la voix vraiment s'adresse
                              et c'est plus
que du chant. Souvenez-vous, nous avions contemplé
dans sa vitrine la Royale la galère rouge
et l'or du Roi-Soleil sur les vagues de carton pâle
qui s'effaçaient avec l'histoire des rameurs sans paroles
                      n'étaient ces bribes de chansons
obscènes et douces que vous m'aviez,
me surprenant, citées. Puis nous avions marché
dans le temps travesti de septembre ;
aux Tuileries les poissons viennent guetter le pain
et leur bassin reste un repère du cœur léger. « Oï-ho !
c'est une brise,
                      disiez-vous jouant de votre jupe,
qui fait gonfler même les mâts ! » Votre visage
souriait : « C'est de l'érudition, monsieur. Donnez
donc votre main, nous allons boire un chocolat
chez moi et n'ayez crainte, pour la passion
et ses images, vous en aurez mais après ce que je veux. »

September

The black lamp at the flank of dawn
how much longer will it hold out
with its déjà-vu in the backlit
reverie of words? There are so many other things
equally portentous, more precise: the line
a voice is really aiming at
                              and it's more
than just song. Do you remember, we had been looking
through museum glass at the Sun King's navy, his red galleon
and his gold on waves of pale cardboard
which erased themselves with the oarsmen's stories wordless
        except for those snatches of bawdy
sweet songs which you, surprising me,
had sung. Then we'd walked
in the disguised September weather
through the Tuileries, where fish swam up hunting for crumbs,
and their pond is still a light heart's landmark.
                                        "Heave-ho,
here's a breeze,"
                  you said, smoothing down your skirt,
"that will stiffen even the masts." Your face
was all smiles. "That's erudition, sir. Give me
your hand, we'll go drink some hot chocolate
at my place, and don't worry, as for passion
and its metaphors, you'll have all you like, but after what I want."

Loin de Byzance

Joseph Brodsky

L'AME DE VICTIME
Avait largement reçu de quoi
Devenir un perroquet doloriste,
Mais un jour il a vidé ses placards
Des habits qui auraient trop bien
Convenu à l'ennemi, et il est parti
Vers un vent d'au-delà des terres.
Les juges, il les a laissés vieillir
De plus en plus vite, avec le souvenir
Du bon vieux temps où l'on bandait même
Devant *L'Inscription de la jeune fille*
Au Komsomol. A ceux qui voulaient sa veste
Il a laissé son manteau : la victoire,
Messieurs, c'est de ne jamais laisser
La belle *âme de victime* rafler la mise.

Far from Byzantium

For Joseph Brodsky

A VICTIM'S SOUL
Had received more than enough to make
Of him a grief-glorifying parakeet,
But one day he emptied his closets
Of suits which would have been all too
Becoming to the enemy, and he went off
Toward a wind from beyond those lands.
As for the judges, he left them to age
More and more quickly, with the memory
Of the good old days when they got a hard-on even
In front of *The Young Girl Being Registered
In the Komsomol*. To those who wanted his jacket
He left his coat: victory
My good sirs, is never to allow
The noble *victim's soul* to walk off with the jackpot.

Le mètre et le chagrin

Moteur du discours ? La langue elle-même,
La masse des vers qui moud le thème
Et ressac soudain, sur une rime
Un accent. On n'arrête pas le temps
Messieurs, on peut essayer de le compter
A sa manière, avec des sons, sur les doigts
Seulement de la main, tandis que la méchanceté
Choisit toujours les grands nombres.
« Garde tes larmes, disait très tôt la mère,
Pour des choses plus graves. » Poésie,
Le chagrin contenu par le mètre.

Meter and Grief

The driving force of the discourse? Language itself,
The mass of verses which grind up the theme
And sudden backwash, on a rhyme,
An accent. One doesn't stop time,
Good sirs, but one can try to count it
One's own way, with sounds, on the fingers
Of one's hands, while wickedness
Inevitably chooses large numbers.
"Save your tears," his mother told him early on,
"For more serious things." Poetry,
Grief contained by meter.

La pièce d'or

Panique en route (l'herbe n'a jamais
Eté d'office ennemie du bourreau)
Et faire de la panique la *limite acoustique*
Du mot. Désespoir et distance... C'est
A la vitesse de créer le sujet, même si
Certains font déjà bouffer les rats
Pour sauver les provisions. *Ne pense jamais
A ce que tu as dépensé :* rester ce temps
Qu'on ne rattrape pas, ce *presque,*
Ni adulte ni enfant, ce *on moins qu'un.*
Sur la rétine, une seule pièce d'or
Suffira *pour toute la longueur des ténèbres.*

The Gold Piece

Panic en route (the grass is not necessarily
Always the executioner's enemy),
And then to make panic the *sound barrier*
Of the word. Despair and distance . . . It's speed
That creates the subject, even if
Some are already eating rats
To economize their provisions. *Never think*
About what you have spent: how to be that time
For which one never makes up, that *almost*
Neither child nor adult, that *next-to-nobody?*
On the retina, a single gold piece
Will suffice *for the whole length of darkness.*

Le double

Le geste de la main sur le front quand la chaleur
est mauvaise ; le même quand jeune il balayait
la classe pour du vieux pain, tâchait d'apprendre
par cœur les lettres du tableau laissé. Maintenant
que la sueur est plus forte encore, c'est la bouche
qui se crispe ; il sait pourtant que ce n'est pas
cette maladie venue plus tard en goinfrerie
du trop de sucre, mais l'aiguille qui devait soulager,
mais souillée par la septicémie sans erreur des prisons.
C'est presque aussi la même folie de poussière
dans le même rayon de soleil,

                      mais sans la promesse
des étrangères au champ de courses,
l'étreinte récompense des nouveaux princes
dociles. Et toujours la même question : à quel âge
devient-on tyran, et durable champion de la foire
aux tyrans ? Lui meurt au-dessus des latrines,
se doute qu'un jour celui qui le remplace
au palais finira en délire nerveux de vieillard,
et par la fenêtre de la cellule, il les voit,
elle lui a caressé les cheveux, ils repartent,
son double ancien, l'enfant qui vient de ramasser la boîte
vide, et sa mère l'encore timide femme-mendiante.

The Double

His hand's movement to his forehead when the heat's
oppressive; the same as when, in his youth, he swept
the classroom in exchange for stale bread, trying
to learn the letters left on the blackboard by heart. Now
that the sweat is even more profuse, it's his lips
that clench; all the same he knows that it isn't
from the sickness he caught later out of gluttony
for sugar, but from the needle which should soothe,
soiled now by the unerring septicemia of prisons.
It's almost the same dusty madness
in the same sunbeam,

                          but without the promise
of foreign women at the racetrack,
the embrace rewarding new and docile
princes. And always the same question: at what age
does one become a tyrant, enduring champion in the tyrant
show? He is dying in the latrines,
suspects that his replacement in the palace will
end his days in an old man's feverish delirium,
and out the cell window he sees them,
she has stroked his hair, they leave again,
his former double, the child who just picked up the empty
box, and his mother, the still-timid beggar woman.

Les chiens

Il nous aimait, avec nos gueules, nos crocs,
L'attaque au moindre bruit de pas, de grincement
De porte : la trique et la gamelle, de quoi
Prendre des forces mais jamais l'avant-goût
Du paradis des chiens, le sucre par plaisir,
L'instant tout seul. La bonne chère, c'était
Pour lui : faisait la fête, chantait aux larmes,
Rond comme queue de pelle sous la lune, doublait
Sa graisse à toutes ventrées, bâfrait la viande
Et les patates avec la sauce, bâfrait
Tous les fromages entre deux trous normands,
Et puis le croustillant du caramel, la pièce montée
Meringue à fond de kirsch, la crème comme éternelle
Ecume : un soir, à son retour on l'a bouffé.

The Dogs

He loved us, with our muzzles and our fangs,
How we'd surge at the slightest footstep, creak
Of a door: truncheon and trough, enough
To gather your strength, but never a foretaste
Of dog paradise, sugar for pleasure,
An instant for itself. Fine food was all
For him: partied, sang his heart out,
Round as a spade handle in the moonlight, doubled
His fat by the bellyful, gobbled up meat
And potatoes in sauce, gobbled up all
The cheeses between two shots of Calvados,
And then the caramel-crisp masterpiece,
Kirsch-flavored meringue, cream like eternal
Sea foam: one night, when he came home, we wolfed him down.

Le veilleur

La Patrie reconnaissante
Lui renouvelle tous les six ans
Sa prothèse et le rend ensuite
A une sagesse de caporal-chef
Qui n'est pas la sienne : il voulait
Etre instituteur, médecin
Ou grand-père dans un pays
De terres brunes, et d'hirondelles
Tissant au moindre contre-jour
D'immenses trames de rêves.
A sa fenêtre il guette le moment
Où les lampes vont s'éteindre
Dans la nuit plate et sans air
Il a confiance il aura le dernier cri.

The Night Watchman

In gratitude, every six years
The Homeland sends him a new
Prosthesis, thus returning him to
A corporal's wisdom, which is not at all
His own: he had wanted to be
A schoolmaster, a doctor,
Or a grandfather in a country
Of brown earth and of swallows
Weaving against the slightest backlight
A vast fabric of dreams.
At his window, he watches for the moment
When the streetlights go out
In the flat and airless night.
He knows the last cry will be his own.

PROMENADE EN VILLE :: A WALK IN THE CITY

La librairie du Scarabée

Comme sur le perron d'un rêve,
La jupe rose, un nœud dans les cheveux,
A soixante ans « *t'as pas cent balles* »
Réclame-t-elle à celui qui regarde
Sa jeunesse dans les livres anciens,
Le voyage de Babar, Mitchi
L'ourson sans mère dans la vitrine,
Avec derrière l'épaule les vieux
Amours venus rôder au bord
De la Montagne Sainte-Geneviève.
Temps où l'on se laissait glisser
Sur son ombre tandis qu'au reflux
De la mémoire monte en sublime
Odeur un rot d'alcool pas cher.

The Scarab Bookshop

It might be on the front steps of a dream,
Her pink skirt, the ribbon in her hair
At sixty. *Can you spare me a tenner?*
She insists, as you stare
At your own childhood in those old books,
Babar's Journey, Mitchi
The Bearcub, motherless in the window,
While behind your back all of your old
Loves have returned to lurk around
The foot of the Montagne Sainte-Geneviève.
A time when you have let yourself slip
On your own shadow, while on memory's
Ebb tide there rises in sublime
Odiferousness a belch of cheap booze.

Le chauffeur

Qu'est-ce qui rôde autour du chauffeur
Qui a quitté son autobus, s'est assis
Place de l'Opéra au bord du trottoir
Et glisse dans la douceur de n'être
Déjà plus que ses larmes ? Les passants
Qui se penchent sur une tristesse
Commune et présentable aimeraient
Qu'il leur dise que le vent naguère
Savait venir de la forêt vers une robe,
Ou qu'un jour son frère lui a lancé
Même ton ombre ne voudra plus de toi.
Les pieds dans l'eau, le chauffeur
Ne sait que répéter : *ce travail est dur*
Et le monde n'est pas complaisant.

The Bus Driver

What has gotten into the bus driver
Who has left his bus, who has sat down
On a curb on the place de l'Opéra
Where he slips into the ease of being
Nothing more than his own tears? The passersby
Who bend over such a shared and
Presentable sorrow would like him
To tell them that the wind used to know
How to come out of the woods toward a woman's dress,
Or that one day his brother said to him,
Even your shadow wants nothing to do with you.
His feet in a puddle, the bus driver
Can only repeat, *This work is hard
And people aren't kind.*

Arènes de Lutèce

Il n'y a que quelques chaises
Et l'herbe est mouillée
Sous les fesses quand s'élèvent
Les phrases du *Steinway* mais l'artiste
Ce soir est un renard qui n'aura
Pas besoin de faire crier Schubert.
Très haut entre les notes passent
Les avions, la fin d'un grondement
Vient parfois combler la courbe
D'un silence tandis qu'une petite
Fille roule sur sa pente de gazon
Jusqu'à l'estrade autour de laquelle
On se retrouvera pour le champagne
Et les accords brisés pour rire.

Arènes de Lutèce

There are only a few chairs,
And the grass is damp
Beneath our buttocks when the Steinway's
Phrases rise, but the pianist
Tonight is a fox who will not
Need to make Schubert shriek.
High up between the notes the airplanes
Pass by, the tail end of their rumbling
Sometimes fills up the curve
Of a rest, while a little
Girl rolls down her slope of lawn
Right to the edge of the rostrum around which
We'll gather afterward for champagne
And chords jokingly broken.

La République

Soirs d'asphalte mouillé, ivres de *Non,*
Rien de rien..., l'âne et le lion des fêtes
Tournent au manège face à la statue
Dressée sur sa ronde de bas-reliefs :
On y charge par vagues à Valmy,
Une femme à gestes brusques
Rhabille un enfant geignard
Et le *Vengeur* n'en finit pas de couler
Un treize Prairial tandis
Qu'au sommet du limonaire
Des bateaux genevois s'emplissent
De silènes venus lorgner la République
Aux seins lourds qui compte ses clochards
Et ses flics en rêvant son vieux futur.

Place de la République

Nights of wet asphalt, drunk on *Non,*
Je ne regrette rien . . . , the holiday donkey and lion
Revolve on the carousel facing the statue
Erect on its round plinth of bas-reliefs:
Waves of riders charge at Valmy.
With brusque movements a woman pulls
A whining child's coat back on
And the *Vengeur* never stops sinking
On the thirteenth of Prairial while
On the revolving frieze above the animals
Boats from Geneva fill up
With satyrs come to ogle the heavy-
Breasted Republic, who counts her bums
And cops while dreaming up her aged future.

Parc de la Cité

Elle était l'embrassée

D'un maladroit, le firmament

De la nuit d'août versait sur eux

Son lait d'étoiles les pelouses

Etaient encore plus chaudes

Que leur peau le long

De la haie un voyeur

Vu s'enfuyait elle tenait

A découvrir ses seins. Nul

D'entre eux ne connaissait

Le sexe voulaient-ils

Ce mélange d'ardeur et

De gâchis c'est en pleine

Jeunesse qu'ils se quittèrent.

Parc de la Cité

She was being kissed
By a blunderer, the August night's
Firmament poured its
Starry milk down on them the lawn
Was even warmer
Than their skin alongside
The hedge a spied voyeur
Fled she insisted on
Uncovering her breasts. Neither
Of them had ever
Had sex did they want
That mixture of fervor and
Waste it was in the fullness of
Youth that they left each other.

Déesse du Printemps

à Jean-Pierre Lemaire

Le temps s'est effacé où défense
Etait faite de manger du lièvre,
De crainte que ne se transmît
A l'homme la lubricité de cet animal
Nocturne et sodomite qui boxe
Sa compagne avant de la monter.
Les enfants ce matin cherchent
Du chocolat dans l'herbe fraîche,
Et l'Eglise en verve fait retentir
Les cloches d'une Résurrection
Tandis qu'un homme à la recherche
De pièces d'or met au jour les os
Rompus et calcinés d'une prêtresse
D'*Oster,* déesse aux grande hases.

Goddess of Spring

for Jean-Pierre Lemaire

Erased from our annals is the time when
It was forbidden to eat hare for fear
That humans might be infected
With the lechery of that nocturnal
Sodomite of an animal who boxes
With his mate before mounting her.
This morning children are out hunting
For chocolate in the damp grass,
And the church, in top form, sounds out
The bells of a Resurrection
While a man searching for gold
Coins unearths the calcinated bone
Shards of a priestess of *Oster,*
Goddess flanked by giant she-hares.

La demande

Tu travailles pour le fric ou pour
La baise, demande à l'infirmière
Une femme que les policiers amènent,
Prise dans une colère qui n'est déjà
Plus à elle. Elle crie : *les poules*
Du haut finissent toujours par salir
Celles d'en bas, et s'en va
Vers le lit bancal où la chère
Innocence se fait une fois encore
Recoudre le pucelage. *Vous ne voulez*
Jamais sauver, ajoute-t-elle,
Que ce qui est perdu.

                               La télévision,
Ecrit l'interne sur le formulaire,
Semble avoir cessé de l'intéresser.

The Question

Do you work for the dough or to
Get laid, the nurse is asked by
A woman who's brought in by the police,
Seized by a rage that is no longer
Entirely hers. She shouts, *The hens*
On top always end up shitting
On the ones below, and goes off toward
The rickety bed, where her precious
Innocence will have its hymen
Mended once more. *You never*
Want to save anything, she adds,
But what's already lost.
                    Television,
Writes the intern on her chart,
Seems to have stopped interesting her.

Eclaircie

Le soleil réchauffe les bancs de bois
Et les statues aux noms effacés.
A contre-jour entre les arbres,
Une petite fille au violoncelle
Refuse de passer par l'allée
Où depuis un siècle le lion vert
Dévore une autruche. Dans le coin
Des brouettes, Flaubert a l'air
Sur le point d'exploser contre
La bêtise de son propre buste.
Assise sur le bord du bassin,
Une femme retire son pull-over
Sans voir que pendant ce temps
Son amie brune lui regarde les seins.

Jardin du Luxembourg: Bright Interval

Sunlight caresses the wooden benches
And statues with their names effaced.
Backlit between the trees.
Meanwhile a little girl holding a cello
Will not go down the walk
Where, for a century, a green lion
Has been devouring an ostrich. In the corner
For storing wheelbarrows, it seems Flaubert
Is about to burst with rage against
The foolishness of his own portrait bust.
A woman seated at the boat-pond's rim
Tugs her sweater off over her hair
Without noticing that all this time
Her dark-eyed girlfriend's looking at her breasts.

Le bassin

à Laury Granier

L'équinoxe renverse ses effets,
Le vent d'ouest a fini de coucher
En tempête les voiliers à treize francs
Qui coursaient les canards, de jeunes
Moineaux reviennent faire leur trou
Dans le sable sous le banc, ils y laissent
Parfois une plume. *Le harcèlement*
Est un délit, dit une fille au garçon
Sans chaussettes. Un couple d'âge mûr
A repris ses caresses devant le factionnaire
Et les tulipes : la femme a la jambe
Un peu courte et l'homme affirme
Que l'achat de livres sera bientôt un signe
De très forte aliénation mentale.

The Sailboat Pond

for Laury Granier

The equinox reverses its effects,
The west wind has finished flattening
In its storm the sailboats, rented for thirteen francs,
That raced the ducks, some young
Sparrows come back to dig their dust pits
In the sand beneath the bench, they leave
A feather there sometimes. *Harassment*
Is a crime, a girl says to a boy
Wearing no socks. A middle-aged pair
Resume embracing in front of the sentry
And the tulips: the woman is a bit
Short-legged, and the man declares
That buying books will soon become a clear
Sign of derangement, yes, insanity.

Le docteur

Les arbres de la cour circulaire
Jaunissent, une délirante en contention
Les regarde ; elle se met à parler
Soudain comme si de rien n'avait
Jamais été, puis meurt le lendemain
De sa tuberculose en s'excusant
D'avoir tant dérangé. *Il ne faut pas*
Non plus, dit le docteur, *chercher*
A complètement calmer certains
Patients car ils s'ennuieraient trop.
Il a cessé de rêver aux sociétés
Sans classes, et s'installe parfois
Devant le kiosque municipal pour écouter
Une fanfare jouer des marches d'Empire.

The Doctor

In the circular courtyard, trees
Turn yellow, a madwoman in a straitjacket
Watches them; all at once she starts to speak
As if nothing were out of the ordinary,
And the next day she dies
Of tuberculosis, making excuses
For having been such a bother.
It is not necessary, says the doctor,
To try to calm such patients down completely
They would become too bored. He has ceased
Imagining a classless society
And sometimes sits in front of the municipal
Bandshell to listen to a brass band play
Military marches of the Empire.

La réponse

Chaque avancée de nuages plombe
Un peu la coupole aux grands hommes,
Puis elle explose à nouveau
De tout son gris bleu en recevant
Le soleil. Une femme en jupe
Courte et claire est allongée
Sur un fauteuil de métal. Sa main
Tient firme la cuisse de son voisin,
Un garçon les regarde et se moque,
En quelques gestes, des fausses
Sorties dominicales ; comme si
C'était du Marivaux, une amie répond
Rondement que les gens *font semblant*
De faire semblant, et c'est vrai.

The Answer

Each forward movement of the clouds leadens
The cupola covering the great men
A bit more. Then it explodes again
In all its blue-gray sheen as it receives
The sun. A woman in a bright-
Colored mini-skirt has stretched herself out
On a metal chair. Her hand
Is planted firmly on her neighbor's thigh.
A boy observing them makes fun,
With brusque gestures, of imitation
Conjugal Sundays; as if it were
A play by Marivaux, a female friend
Briskly replies, *Sometimes people pretend*
To be pretending, and it's true.

Dix-huit heures trente

L'inspecteur général des mines
Suit du regard une partie de tennis
Plutôt maladroite. Il est mort
En mille huit cent quatre-vingt-deux
Après avoir organisé une exposition
Universelle ; au pied de la statue,
Une jeune fille en robe claire
S'est installée à califourchon
Sur les cuisses de son ami
Qu'elle fait semblant de violer.
Dans l'air qui vient les rafraîchir
En apportant les odeurs du verger
Et des échos de discussion sur le chômage,
Le garçon résiste à petits cris.

Six-Thirty

The inspector general of mines
Follows a badly played
Tennis match with his eyes. He died
In eighteen eighty-two
After having organized
A world's fair. At the foot of the statue
An adolescent in a summer dress
Has seated herself astride
Her boyfriend's thighs
And pretends to rape
Him. In the late afternoon air
Come to cool them with an orchard's odor
And echoed words on joblessness and labor,
The boy resists, emitting little cries.

Bacchus

Les sexes sont cachés par des étoffes
En érection, et le dieu de métal
A gros plis s'esclaffe en lorgnant
Un groupe de collégiens qui l'ignorent
Et font leur gymnastique au son
D'un sifflet à roulette. *En petites*
Foulées ! dit la maîtresse, devant
Les trois bacchantes qui roulent
Dans l'air froid, jambes éparpillées
Sous le bourricot. Pour faire frémir
Sa camarade, un garçon lui affirme
Nous, hier on a mangé du kangourou
Puis s'éloigne dans le bruit
Des aspirateurs à feuilles mortes.

Bacchus

Their genitals are hidden by tumescent
Fabric, and the metal god
With his deep pleats chortles as he ogles
A band of twelve-year-olds who ignore him
And perform their gymnastics to the sound
Of a blown whistle. *Take small*
Steps! says the gym teacher, in front of
The three bacchantes who roll
In the cold air, their legs splayed out
Under the god's donkey. To make his classmate
Shudder, a boy assures her,
At our house last night we ate kangaroo,
Then wanders away in the noise
Of vacuum cleaners sucking up dead leaves.

Verlaine

à Guy Goffette

Verlaine ? Il est dressé sur l'herbe,
Lyre et palme dans le dos, Verlaine,
En buste, au sommet de trois bons
Mètres de pine granitique où se tordent
D'improbables muses affolées d'être
Prises en sa compagnie sous le regard
De promeneurs peu regardants
Aux combats du plaisir. Le hurlement
Amer d'une moto trouble soudain
Le petit chant de pluie sur les platanes
Et châtaigniers, un rayon de soleil
Tranche en clair-obscur le massif rouge
Et vert, et Verlaine renfrogné rêve encore
L'air qui ferait tout tenir ensemble.

Verlaine

for Guy Goffette

Verlaine? He stands erect there on the grass,
Lyre and palm tree behind him, a bronze bust
Of Verlaine atop three good yards
Of cement prick around which writhe three
Unlikely Muses, panic stricken to be
Discovered in such dubious company
By strollers so much less interested
In amorous combat. The bitter roar
Of a motorcycle rudely interferes
With the rain's small music beneath the plane
Trees and chestnuts; a ray of sun
Slices to chiaroscuro the red and green
Bushes, and sulking Verlaine still dreams
The air that will make everything cohere.

La chiffonnerie

Il y a suffisamment d'arbres
Nus, de silhouettes pauvres
Dans le parc pour se payer la pointe
D'une mélancolie en compagnie
De quelques dieux qui paillardent
A tout hasard dans la chiffonnerie
Du cœur et rigolent en contre thème
Quand on double deux passantes
Vêtues de jaune et gris
Et qu'on entend l'une dire à la plus
Vieille un peu cassée qu'une voisine
Est morte il y a deux jours
A quatre-vingt-sept ans, et l'autre
De répondre : *Ah, ça c'est bien !*

The Rag-and-Bone Shop

There are enough stark-naked
Trees, impoverished silhouettes
In the park to treat oneself to a spot
Of melancholy in the company
Of a few gods partying
On the off chance in the rag-and-bone shop
Of the heart and laughing in counterpoint
When you go past two women walking
Dressed in yellow and gray
And hear one of them say to the older,
Somewhat stooped one that a neighbor died
Two days ago at the age of eighty-seven,
And the other answer, *Ah, now that's not bad!*

La petite troupe

Ayant perdu son fils, le professeur
De philosophie continuait à se demander
Si la fin de l'illusion pouvait
Se passer de colère, et il travaillait
Pour que les heures ne soient pas
Toutes semblables. Quand le printemps
S'attardait au jardin du Luxembourg
Entre garçons et filles, il passait
Dans l'ombre des reines de France
Pour rafler les volontaires du jour
Et une troupe enjouée montait
Alors la rue Soufflot, entourant celui
Qui pardonnait sa vigueur à la jeunesse
Et mourut peu après sa retraite.

The Little Band

After the death of his son, the professor
Of philosophy continued asking
Himself if the end of illusion could
Be achieved without anger, and he worked
So that every hour did not seem identical
To every other. When spring
Lingered in the Luxembourg Gardens
Between boys and girls, he used to pass
Beneath the shadows of the queens of France
Gathering up the day's volunteers
And a joyous band would then
Ascend the rue Soufflot, around the one
Who pardoned youth its vigor
And died shortly after he retired.

Rue de Tournon

Joseph Roth

Une jeune fille vint le voir, tenant
Un chapeau de paille qui rappelait
Grillons et coquelicots, puis
La guerre détruisit le vieil Empire
Où la justice renonçait parfois
Aux dents du dragon. Plus tard,
L'ombre des cheminées s'avança, cri
Après cri, sur la vie en fuite
Jusqu'à cette rue de grand cardinal
Où l'alcool se filtrait dans sa propre
Ironie. Devant sa plaque, la mémoire
Cherche les éclairs qu'il savait
Pourtant faire surgir des jeux d'ombre
Et lumière sur la pierre des villes.

Rue de Tournon

Joseph Roth

A young girl once came to see him; in her hand
Was a straw hat, reminder of
Crickets and poppies; then
War destroyed the ancient empire
Where justice occasionally renounced
Its dragon's teeth. Later on
Shadows of the chimneys, cry after cry,
Caught up with life, which fled
Here to the street named for a cardinal
While alcohol seeped through his own
Irony. Examining his plaque, memory
Searches for those bursts of light which he
Could nonetheless draw from the play
Of light and shadow on cities' stone.

Le *Frisbee*

L'œil ne lâche plus le disque
Qui rebondit au sol, déchire
Le feuillage de tout son rouge
Et pivote au bout d'un doigt
Avant que la main ne le relance
A tout vent vers une fille
Aux cheveux de renard : elle le saisit
En lui tournant le dos et l'envoie
Au diable dans une spirale de bras,
De hanches qui luttent à leur façon
Contre le froid, avant l'heure
Du thé au rhum qu'on boira devant
Les petites lampes du bistrot
Faites pour le calme des visages.

The Frisbee

Your eye doesn't leave the disk
Which bounces on the ground, rips
Through the foliage with its total red
And pivots to a fingertip
Before the hand releases it
Full tilt toward a girl
With foxy hair: she seizes it
From behind her back and sends it
Straight to hell in a spiral of arms
And hips which struggle in their own way
Against the cold, before the hour
Comes to drink tea with rum in front of
The little bistro lamps
Made for the calm they spill on faces.

Quai des Orfèvres

Martin Flinker

Le petit homme fermait parfois
Sa librairie, le temps de recopier
Un inédit qu'on récitait. « Etonnant,
Ce poème, *weiss sind die Tulpen,* ça vient
De Rilke, j'en suis sûr, *schwartz sind*
Die Straücher, mais il a mis *tulipes blanches*
Au lieu de *sapins noirs :* Paul
Celan n'aimait pas les grands arbres. Vous
Ne l'avez pas connu, et vous aimez ?
Attention à la bigoterie ! Ici, c'est
La fosse aux livres, et les gens
En vitrine sont presque tous des amis
Morts : la littérature, ça n'est
Jamais qu'une façon de passer. »

Quai des Orfèvres

Martin Flinker

The little man would sometimes shut
His bookshop long enough to copy out
An unpublished one we'd read out loud. "Surprising,
This poem, *weiss sind die Tulpen,* that comes
From Rilke, I'm sure of it, *schwartz sind
Die Sträucher,* but he's put *white tulips*
Instead of *black firs:* Paul
Celan didn't like tall trees. You
Never knew him, and you like these poems?
Watch out for bigotry! Here it's
A mass grave for books, and the people
In the window are almost all dead
Friends: literature, all it is ever
Is a way to pass, get by."

La meule

à Jacques Réda

Déjà debout, bouclant une conversation
Sur *Le Vallon* où coulent deux ruisseaux
Qui meurent discrètement sous l'herbe,
Pour laisser courir en parallèle l'*âme*
Et le *cœur* du poème, chacun serrant
Au fil des strophes sa double part
D'enfance et de temps malmené. Alors,
Il met un casque rouge, sorti d'un film
Où la Loren vous prenait à bras-le-corps
En lançant la jambe vers les braguettes
Du public avide, et quand il a filé
Sur sa meule aiguisant le canif à césures,
Il faut guetter son chant dans les échos
Qui roulent entre la Butte et Gambetta.

The Moped

for Jacques Réda

Already standing, tying up a conversation
About *The Valley,* where two streams flow
Which expire discreetly beneath the grass,
So as to let run parallel *the soul*
And *the heart* of the poem, as the stanzas unroll
Each of them seizing his double portion
Of childhood and misspent time. Then
He puts on a red helmet, straight out of a film,
Where Loren seizes you head-on
Thrusting her leg out toward the trouser flies
Of her avid public, and when he has gone off
On his moped, his caesura cutter sharpened,
You must listen for his singing in the echoes
That roll between Gambetta and the Butte.

L'ombre

Le *cutter* fait une dernière entaille
Dans le marron que la main gercée replace
Parmi les autres, au centre du tonneau
Qui sert de réchaud : « *Dix francs !* »
Dit le marchand à l'heure du loup,
Près de la plaque de marbre
Du pont-des-Arts, qui parle
D'ouvriers du Livre et de mort.
Sur la façade des bâtiments d'Etat,
Le projecteur d'un bateau-mouche
En contrebas projette en ombres
Gigantesques les bonnets
Et casquettes des derniers bouquinistes
Qui achèvent de fermer leurs coffres.

The Shadow

The cutter makes a last slice
In a chestnut which the chapped hand places
Among the others in the middle of the tin barrel
In which they're heated: "*Ten francs!*"
Cries the vendor in encroaching dusk
Near the marble plaque
On the pont des Arts, which speaks
Of workers in the book arts, and of death.
On the facades of state office buildings
The light projector of a bateau-mouche
Below throws up in giant
Shadows the knitted hats
And caps of the last booksellers,
Who are shutting up shop.

Sérénade

L'ennui, dans le métro, gravite
Au foie du passant pressé
Qui enjambe un clochard
Et bouscule une femme aux allures
De gourde entretenue pour
Pas trop cher : elle lui jette
Le fiel qu'elle achète à ses maîtres
Et il la retrouvera au guichet
Du conservatoire où l'on joue,
Dans des allures de miracle,
La *Sérénade* de Schönberg. Elle n'a
Pourtant rien de si radieux,
Se dit-il en rentrant par les quais
Que le brouillard peuple d'ombres.

Serenade

In the subway, boredom prowls
Around the liver of a rushed commuter
Who steps over a bum
And jostles a woman with the air
Of a lady kept on the cheap.
She turns toward him and tosses
Back the bile she buys from her bosses
And he'll find her later behind the ticket window
Of the conservatory, where they are playing
Schoenberg's *Serenade,* with the air
Of a miracle. There's
Nothing that radiant about it, though,
He thinks, as he walks home along the quays
That the fog is peopling with shadows.

Supermarché

Chocolats, bière, pâtés, whisky,
Gâteaux, elle les regarde se gaver
Et la fille déjà saoule, un rouge
Vif, l'insulte, veut lui casser
Sa gueule de vioque, ils rient,
Ils crient *voleuse,* les gardes
Arrivent, la touchent, les autres rient
Plus fort ; elle lâche : *Pas moi ! C'est eux !*
Les gardes fouillent, la fille lui saute
Dessus, les gardes tapent et les flics
Tapent, ça tape encore dans le bureau
Du directeur, les gars menacent, la fille
La griffe, elle fuit, le directeur la suit,
Lui crie : *Madame, vous oubliez la prime !*

The Supermarket

Chocolates, beer, pâtés, whiskey,
cookies, she watches them stuff it away
and the girl, already drunk, bright
red, insults her, threatens to sock
her in the face, old bag, they laugh,
they shout, *Thief!* The security guards
come, grab her, the others laugh
harder; she exclaims, *Not me! It's them!*
The guards frisk them, the girl
jumps on her, the guards hit,
the cops hit, there's more roughing up
in the manager's office, the guys threaten her, the girl
scratches her, she runs away, the manager follows her,
shouting, *Lady, you forgot your reward!*

Tête de nœud

Tête de nœud porte *jean* tête de nœud
Porte bleu il écrit pour être
Ecrivain écrit qu'il est écrivain
Et fait écrire par les copains
Qu'il n'y a pas plus écrivain
Comme le dit la photo c'est une face
D'écrivain à façons d'écriture
Qui sourit au destin dur et puis
Se rue sur son sourire et lui roule
Des pelles, ou gratte ses griffures
Au bord du précipice pour faire
Taire le monde pendant qu'il souffre
De sa solitude et louche, un œil
Sur le néant et l'autre sur la presse.

Knothead

Knothead wears jeans knothead
Wears blue he writes to be
A writer writes that he is a writer
And gets his pals to write
That no one could be more a writer
His photo says it all it's the face
Of a writer with a flair for writing
Who smiles at grim fate and then
Pounces on his smile and slobbers
It with kisses or scratches his scribbles
At the precipice's edge to make
The world shut up while he suffers
From solitude and squints, one eye
On nothingness the other on the press.

La tentation derrière l'église

La flamme rousse du sucre candi
Explose entre les *jésuites* pansus
Les flacons de Grand Marnier
Et les tartes à la crème habillées
Pour dimanche. Il peut arriver
Quand midi sonne au clocher de l'église
Qu'une femme plonge un bras
Au duvet clair parmi de petits canards
A goût d'amande et vous les fasse
Humer à même sa peau.
On paie, un œil sur sa poitrine,
Et l'on redescend dans le métro
Devant le type qui gueule encore :
L'heure approche, repentez-vous !

Temptation Behind the Church

The reddish flame of candied sugar
Bursts out among the paunchy *Jesuits,*
The flasks of Grand Marnier
And whipped-cream pies decked out
For Sunday. It sometimes happens
When the church clock strikes noon
That a woman thrusts her downy blond
Arm among the marzipan
Ducks and has you
Sniff them right against her skin.
You pay, while eyeing her chest,
And go back down into the metro
In front of the fellow still shouting,
Repent, for the hour is near!

Fenêtre sur cour

C'est cela : une crispation du corps
Face à la rambarde avant que les yeux
Ne plongent vers le bas. La lumière
De fin d'après-midi attendrit la pierre
Et les volets entrebâillées d'où partent
Des voix de travailleurs au noir
Qui refont un parquet en s'engueulant.
— *Quand tu étais petite,* soutient
Dans la cour une mère, *tu étais
Bien plus gentille.* L'enfant répond :
Je te connaissais moins, et s'en va
Jouer dans l'angle à géraniums
Avec le monde de comptines
Que ses doigts glissent entre les mots.

Rear Window

It's just that: your body's contraction
In front of the window guard before your eyes
Can dive toward what's below. The late
Afternoon light gentles the stone
And the half-open shutters, from which emerge
The voices of moonlighting workmen
Who are laying a parquet and quarreling.
— *When you were little,* asserts a mother
In the courtyard, *you were*
Much nicer. The child replies,
I didn't know you so well, and she goes off
To play beside the geranium bed
With the world of nursery rhymes
That her fingers slip in between the words.

VARIATIONS :: VARIATIONS

Acquis

Rêve que la nuit martèle aux portes : ce ne sera
guère plus divertissant que la lecture
d'un de ces livres où l'on appelle angoisse
la trouille d'un anniversaire. *Moi,* disait-elle,
quand je vais au théâtre c'est pour le plaisir
de la rampe et des feux ; je n'aime pas
les porte-parole, ni l'âge où l'on croit
apprendre par effondrements. C'était la terrasse
de Chaillot, à peine oubliée mais si difficile
à saisir : te voilà réduit à d'imperceptibles
acquis, longtemps après, mais sans avoir vécu
les mousquetaires. Et deux petites filles
se battent à qui conservera le mois passé
du calendrier *non l'autre j'en veux pas*
d'abord c'est un crocodile ! Et comment ne pas
rire de ce qui se passe à l'extérieur quand une main,
même avec un peu de chocolat, vous agrippe la manche.

Homilies

Dream that the night is pounding on your door: that would
hardly be more diverting than reading
one of those books in which anguish
is the fear that comes with birthdays. *As for me,* she said,
when I go to the theater, it's for the pleasure
of footlights and chandeliers; I don't like
mouthpieces, or the age when you think
dejection is instructive. It was on the terrace
at Chaillot, barely forgotten but so hard
to grasp: there you are, reduced to intangible
homilies, years later, but without living out
a cloak-and-dagger tale. And two small girls
fight over who'll keep last month's calendar
page: *No I don't want the other one,*
it's a crocodile! And how can you not
laugh at what's going on around you when a hand
even slightly chocolate stained clutches your sleeve.

Le cauchemar

On a pillé son printemps, on continue
Avec celui des autres, on se lève,
On se cogne, on va dans la cuisine
Reprendre un peu de cassoulet froid,
Une bière : par la fenêtre il suffit
De contempler la nuit, la lune
Qu'on dit pétrir un bleu plus pur,
Pour retrouver le sentier des douanes
Et celles qui brûlent dans le feuillage,
L'eau du songe, et le cri sans retour
A la frontière des fous. Pensée serait alors
Ce lien furtif entre les mots, le diable,
Et les jeux de toujours, au bord de l'ombre
Que met pourtant à vif ce cauchemar du poète :
Non pas quand il entend monter,
Dans la ménagerie de ses splendeurs,
Les femmes ou les idées auxquelles
Il a menti, mais quand il réalise
Qu'elles n'étaient jamais dupes.

The Nightmare

You've pillaged your springtime, you'll go on
With someone else's, you get up,
You bump into things, you go into the kitchen
And take a little more cold cassoulet,
A beer: out the window, it's enough
To gaze at the sky, the moon,
Which seems to be kneading a purer blue,
To rediscover the smugglers' trail
And the women burning in the bushes,
The dream waters, and the cry of no return
At the border of madness. Thought, now, would be
That furtive link between words, the devil,
And those perpetual games on the edge of a shadow
Which somehow spotlights the poet's nightmare:
Not when he hears, climbing into
The menagerie of his magnificence
The ideas or the women to whom
He lied, but when he realizes
That they never did believe him.

La vérité

pour Iris et Gérard

Un goût de pommes au miel, de petit
Acide accompagne les larmes lourdes
Du vin, et son ambre à reflets verts
Parle d'anciens automnes. Entre nature
Et temps, au jour de fête, le débat
S'est rouvert, tandis qu'un convive
Remarque : *Si Voltaire écrit des contes*
C'est que la vérité pour être comprise
Doit d'abord être crue. Sur le tapis
Devant la cheminée dort une chatte
Qu'on enjambe doucement pour apporter
Les tranches de pain tiède, la terrine
De bécasse mélangée au foie gras,
Aux pistaches concassées à la main.

Truth

for Iris and Gérard

A taste of honeyed apples and of something
Slightly acid escorts the heavy tears
Of wine, and its green-reflected amber
Speaks of long-past autumns. The debate
Between nature and time has been
Reopened this feast day, when a dinner guest
Remarks, *If Voltaire writes tales*
It's because truth, in order to be understood,
Must first be believed. On the carpet
In front of the fireplace dozes
A cat we must step over carefully
To bring the sliced warm bread, the terrine
Of woodcock and foie gras
With hand-ground pistachios.

Fruits sur la fenêtre

Alors le jour, montant du fond bleuté du lac,
Vient aux fenêtres et le silence
Prend cette forme des fruits
Alignés par la chance, tandis que tremble

A contre-champ la fente d'une pêche douce
Qui parle d'heures passées à boire un air
Tiédi dans le cristal sans poison de septembre.
Collines... le ruisseau fait son bruit de captif

Sous les rondins dorés, l'heure avance
Sur un fil de soleil ; de folles captures
Font aussi danser l'herbe, un être humain

Se dit qu'il n'habite qu'une moitié
De lui-même, mais la mesure, qui est unique,
L'empêche de faire de ses remords un balcon.

Fruit on the Windowsill

And then day, rising from the lake's blue depths
Comes to the windows and silence
Takes this form: fruit
Lined up here by chance, while a sweet

Peach's cleft trembles at a reverse angle,
Recalling hours passed drinking air
Warmed in September's unpoisoned crystal.
Hills, and the stream makes its captive sound

Beneath gilt logs, the hour moves forward
On a thread of sun; wild catches
Make the grass dance too, a human being

Reflects that he merely inhabits
Half of himself, but the measure, which is unique,
Keeps him from making a terrace of his regret.

Les pommettes

La main fait glisser une légère
Bretelle noire le long de l'épaule
Trempée de pluie, et la ville
Sous le vent devient l'égale
Des gestes les plus clairs.
Réjouissons-nous un instant
De croire à la figure, récite
La femme aux pommettes saillantes,
Alors qu'à petits pas les montres
Vont leur chemin dans le jour
Véritable. Elle fut la première
A embrasser, et se surprend encore
De sa douceur en regardant sa jambe
Monter vers le vieux lustre.

High Cheekbones

A hand slides the narrow black
Satin strap down a shoulder
Drenched with rain, and the city
Beneath the wind becomes equal to
The most transparent gestures.
Let us rejoice for an instant
That we believe in a face, recites
The woman with high cheekbones,
While step by tiny step watches
Make their way across the veritable
Day. She was the first
To kiss and is still surprising herself
With her own sweetness as she watches her leg
Rise toward the antique chandelier.

Le vin nouveau

Le soleil allume en clair-obscur
L'ombre du frêne dans l'ombre d'or
Du petit bois ; les vitraux
De l'église aux histoires mortes
Vibrent sous le rire des cloches,
Et l'ample robe d'une femme
En aventure fait au passage frémir
La saillie du chemin dans les herbes.
Je te quitte parce que tu n'es plus
Personne, a-t-elle dit à son amant
Devant un carafon de vin nouveau
Dont la splendeur réchauffait la pièce.
Elle marche en souriant, laissant
Aussi glisser des larmes sur ses lèvres.

New Wine

The sun highlights the ash tree's
Shadow against the golden shadow
Of the grove; the stained-glass windows
In the church of defunct histories
Vibrate beneath the laughter of the bells,
And the full skirt of an adventurous
Woman passing by makes the edges
Of the path in the meadow shiver.
I'm leaving you because you aren't
Anybody anymore, she had told her lover
Over a carafe of new wine
Whose brilliance reheated the room.
She walks on smiling, all the time allowing
Tears to glide down across her lips.

Insecte

Chambre, où le papillon de nuit
Hésite autour du damier ocre et bleu :
La lumière d'une lampe tempête
Fait alors danser la croupe de celle
Qui le pourchasse, les pieds nus
Sur le lit, puis la dalle. La fille
A des gestes de fouet inoffensif
Et fébrile, dans le grand miroir
Où tu l'observes quand les hanches
Ajoutent des creux d'ombre
Au tissu doré des murs. Puis, lampe
Soufflée, la course affolée de l'insecte
Traverse l'embrasure vers l'épaisse
Toison d'étoiles où basculera le sommeil.

Insect

Bedroom, in which a moth hesitates
Above the blue and ocher checkerboard.
The light of a hurricane lamp
Makes her buttocks glisten as
She pursues the insect barefoot
Across the bed, then on the tiles. She
Makes futile agitated whipping
Gestures in the oval mirror, where
You watch her as her haunches add
Crevices of shadow to the gilt
Fabric of the walls. Then, the lamp blown
Out, the insect's crazed flight crosses
The window frame toward the thick fleece
Of stars in which sleep will topple down.

Evolène

Frôlée soudain par l'ombre
De ce qu'elle a dit *ça me fait*
Chaud au cœur elle se tait laisse
Jouer la rumeur des autres tables
Où minute par minute se produit
La folie d'être ensemble pour
Un soir avec du vin
Et des gnocchis ; quelqu'un
Au loin proclame qu'on ne doit
Jamais manger l'amour
Sous forme de tripes froides
Elle rit, n'ajoute rien, ne parle surtout
Pas de ce que feint le verre
Qu'elle tient à hauteur de sa gorge.

Evolène

Brushed suddenly by the shadow
Of what she's just said, *That heats up*
My heart, she falls silent, lets
The murmur from the other tables play
While each minute it becomes clearly madder
That they should be here together for
An evening of wine and
Gnocchi. Someone far
Off proclaims that one should never
Ingest love
In the form of cold tripe.
She laughs, adds nothing, certainly doesn't
Speak of what the glass is hiding
That she holds level with her breasts.

La pocharde

L'aubier, l'orant, l'inengendré... Alors, *petit fou !*
disait-elle, petit fou seulement, car *grand fou*
c'est la réponse, à Cavaillon, des melons les plus mûrs
à celui qui les renifle pour choisir. C'est au fond
moins obscène que les *pointes initiantes*
de l'Inexplorable sondant l'Origine que certains
voudraient échanger contre une attestation
de bonnes mœurs poétiques. Mais ceux-là
se feraient plutôt couper en morceaux, telles
dans les années vingt les hystériques
sous le bistouri du chirurgien rapprocheur-de-clitoris,
plutôt que de connaître leur part de vérité.
Et quand elle était mécontente des éloges
que les hommes faisaient d'une autre femme,
elle prenait deux poires par la tige
et les mettait sur sa poitrine : *Comme ça,*
elle les a ! comme ça ! Elles seraient belles,
vos cravates de notaire ! Mais cette fois,
l'échange des rires ou de quelque autre bien
apparemment gratuit comme par exemple l'histoire
du vieux bélier poursuivi par le chien du voisin,
et qu'il avait fallu récupérer dans la mare et réchauffer
devant l'âtre, qui en a vu d'autres, et c'est grandiose
un mouton sec enfin sur pattes qui marche vers la sortie
et le plomb indécis de l'orage en rotant

The Drunkard

The sapwood, the praying figure, the unengendered . . . Well then,
  little fool,
she'd say, only little fool, because *big fool*
is the comeback, in Cavaillon, from the ripest melons
to those who sniff them, choosing. After all,
it's less obscene than the *initiating points*
of the Inexplorable sounding the Origin which certain individuals
would exchange for certification
of their poetic good behavior. But that lot
would rather let themselves be snipped to bits
like hysterics in the '20s under the scalpel
of a clitoris-clipping surgeon
than know their share of the truth.
And when she was unhappy with the praise
men lavished on other women
she'd take two pears by the stems
and hold them to her chest. *Hers are*
just like that, like that! They'll be lovely,
your notary's neckties! But this time
the seemingly free exchange of laughter
or some other goods, like for example the story
of the old ram chased by a neighbor's dog
that we had to haul out of the pond and dry off
in front of the hearth, which had seen some sights, and it's quite a
  sight
a dry sheep back on its feet at last walking toward the door
and the indecisive leaden storm

son biberon sucré de lait-calva, rien de tout cela
n'aurait suffi, et peut-être est-elle repartie
vers les espaces assourdissants et poreux des immeubles
simplement parce qu'elle a cru qu'ici, non seulement
les femmes mais même les pruniers du paysage
avaient fini par vouloir sa perte ; et elle dort,
pocharde céleste, en cotillons sur le toit de sa voiture,
presque rassurée par cette nouvelle hypothèse
de la physique contemporaine qui veut que l'univers
repose sur d'infimes cordes comme au fuseau
de leur son fondamental, et non plus sur l'angoisse
erratique des particules et des amants : c'est un peu
compliqué mais elle dort sur le toit de sa voiture,
là où toujours on aboutit quand on vient d'un balcon.
Air des grandes villes, qui rend libre ! Et Montaigne :
Paris a mon cœur dès mon enfance et je ne suis
français que par cette grande cité. Et pourquoi
se passer la face au vitriol des bons sentiments
quand il suffit de prononcer *ouistiti sexe* pour avoir
l'air d'aller en souriant vers l'être humain
qui n'en demande peut-être pas tant mais est bien obligé
de passer par cette rue où vous l'attendez
sur dix-huit mètres carrés de panneaux multicolores : il a
depuis toujours tellement peur d'arriver en retard.

all the while belching
its baby bottle of calvados-laced milk, even that
wouldn't have been enough, and perhaps she took off again
toward the porous deafening vacant lots between buildings
just because she believed that here not only
the women but even the plum trees in the countryside
had ended up wishing her ill; and she sleeps
in her slip on the roof of her car, celestial drunkard,
almost reassured by that new hypothesis
of contemporary physics which posits the universe
balanced on minute strings as if on the spindle
of their essential sound, and no longer on the erratic
anguish of particles and lovers: it's a bit
complicated, but she sleeps on her car roof,
where you always land when you've walked off a balcony.
The air of big cities, that sets you free! And Montaigne:
My heart has belonged to Paris since childhood, and I am only
French because of that great city, and why
bare your face to the vitriol of good intentions
when you've only to say *cheese* to seem
to go smiling toward some human being
who perhaps doesn't ask for it but is still obliged
to come up that street where you are waiting for him
on eighteen square yards of multicolored panels: he has
always been so afraid of arriving late.

L'ombre tiède

Noir à pois blancs, le tissu
Du pantalon pénètre entre les fesses
Qui connaissent toutes les ruses
De l'ombre tiède ; elles le confisquent,
L'étreignent d'abord par le haut
A la naissance de leur saillie
Et le relâchent un peu, avant
Que les muscles les plus lourds
Ne l'étouffent à nouveau au plus
Profond, pressant, tordant l'un
Après l'autre les plis soyeux
A chaque pas de bête au bord
Du cri, puis la femme se retourne et dit :
Je ne viendrai pas, mon père est mort.

The Warm Shadow

Black with white polka-dots, the fabric
Of her slacks rides up between her buttocks
Which know all the tricks
Of warm shadow, they seize it,
Grasp it at first from above
At the start of their jutting
And then release it a bit, before
The solidest muscles
Stifle it again at the deepest
Declivity, pressing, twisting
The silky folds, one side and then the other
At each step of the beast at the brink
Of a cry, then the woman turns around and says,
I'm not coming, my father died.

Cybèle

Les seins ont pris la vigueur
Des muscles alentour et le ventre
Massif avance en forme de fuseau
Face à l'étagement abrupt
Des vignobles de montagne.
Le soleil incendie les replis
Du bronze et la jambe s'ouvre
Sous le regard des visiteurs
Tandis que tournent les épaules
De nageuse sans tête ; le plus fort
Pour la force vient de ces fesses
De jeune fille rompue aux rites
D'atelier : elles s'acharnent
Sur le socle en tenaille opiniâtre.

Cybele

The breasts have assumed the energy
Of the muscles around them, and the compact
Belly thrusts out tight as a spindle
In front of the steep terraces
Of mountain vineyards.
The sun sets fire to the bronze
Folds, and one leg extends
Under the gaze of visitors
While the headless swimmer's
Shoulders turn away; the power
Culminates in those buttocks
Of a young girl grown used to the studio's
Ceremonies: they hold on
To the plinth like tenacious pincers.

La victime anthropophage

Ariane ma sœur il faut savoir
Les empoigner, ne pas mourir
Comme une conne pour le plaisir
D'un mythe, les tenir serrés
Sous les fesses et ne pas les lâcher
Avant l'ultime soubresaut puis
Les reprendre sur le dos leur dire
De beaux mensonges les guetter
En se guettant soi-même, mordre
Au besoin pour leur montrer
Qu'ils sont aussi le festin d'une bête
Qui aime bras et jambes et leur
Odeur mêlée d'entrailles ils
Ne doivent plus sortir du labyrinthe.

The Anthropophage Victim

Sister Ariadne, you must learn how
To grasp them, not die
Like an ass for the pleasure
Of a myth, hold them tightly
Under the buttocks and not let them go
Before the last shudder then
Take them again on their backs tell them
Lovely lies, keep watch over them
While watching yourself, bite them
If need be to show them
That they also are the feast meat of a beast
Who loves arms and legs and their
Odor mingled with guts they
Must not leave the labyrinth again.

La calomnie d'après Apelle

Aimable est la Vérité quand elle a
Les seins très haut, les doigts fins,
Des cuisses de patineuse et le bonheur
De se heurter à sept greluches
La pire surtout la Pénitence qui
Jouit de se punir et de ne plus marcher
Qu'avec d'innommables pantoufles.
Elle au contraire la fille nue avec l'air
Triste et calme d'une fileuse
Ménage la tempête dans ses hanches
Et c'est elle surtout qu'on veut
Croire quand l'œil s'enroule
Enfin sur ces brins de tabac en nuage
Léger vers l'entrée du bas-ventre.

Slander, After Apelles

Truth is pleasing when she has
High firm breasts, slender fingers,
A skater's thighs, and the good luck
To collide with seven chippies.
The worst of course is Penitence, who
Takes pleasure in self-punishment and walking
From now on only in hideous old slippers.
She, on the other hand, the naked girl with
The calm, sad look of a spinner,
Controls the storm in her hips
And it's she above all you would like
To believe when your eye is reeled in
Finally by those tobacco flakes
In a light cloud below her belly.

Salut l'artiste

A la campagne il lui parle de l'art,
De l'amour, de la vie, il dit qu'il crée,
Qu'il l'aime, elle dit que sa peinture
Est nulle, il dit l'art c'est la vie,
Elle dit qu'il n'est qu'un paresseux,
Il joue à l'agacer avec une herbe, elle
Crie, il dit qu'il va fesser pour la calmer,
Elle le traite de rapin, d'une main il bloque
La nuque, de l'autre il cogne, il rit, elle dit
Que les enfants les voient, il lâche et puis
Le lendemain il la regarde de la rive
Nager les yeux fermés, se dit qu'il est
Heureux d'être avec elle comme il y a
Huit jours au même endroit, mais avec l'autre.

Hail to the Artist

In the country he talks to her about art
About love, about life, he says that he creates
And he loves, she says that his painting
Is rubbish, he says that art is life,
She says that he's a layabout,
He plays at pricking her with a blade of grass, she
Squeals, he says he'll spank her to calm her down,
She calls him a paint dauber, he grabs her neck
With one hand, slaps her with the other, he laughs, she says
The children can see, he lets her go and then
The next day from the riverbank he watches
Her swimming with her eyes closed, says to himself he's
As happy to be with her as he was eight
Days ago, in the same place, but with the other one.

Pas de rimes

Pas d'océan, pas de rimes : la montagne,
prudente, grandes ballades et parfois
quand on se prenait pour de la grandeur,
un grand troupeau bovin, juste avant la gifle
du Mont-Blanc, au revers d'une épaule d'herbe,
on passait au milieu : *N'aie pas peur*
ce ne sont que des vaches ! — Je te dis,
à droite, non, là-bas, il y en avait une,
avec des couilles, où... — Accélère !
elle est juste derrière. Et le soir,
sa culotte rejoignait celle du diable dans
le rire et les odeurs de paille, la vie
dansait comme un vertige d'étoiles mais
seule l'eau n'oublie jamais son chemin,
et dans la ville, après midi, il n'y a
plus de vaches : va lentement
la dame, à distance des années,
sans reconnaître et passe ! tandis que ça
klaksonne à l'Opéra parce qu'un chauffeur d'autobus
pleure dans le caniveau ; reste à chicaner
les souvenirs comme un excommunié, plonger
le nez dans sa *Spaten*, écrire cela
de suite, ce qu'il en reste
est plus fragile que maison d'araignée,
mais on devrait sentir qu'un simple passant
pourrait bien prendre la table à travers la gueule.

No Rhymes

No ocean, no rhymes, the prudent
mountain, long walks, and sometimes
when we thought too highly of ourselves
a huge bovine herd, just before the slap
of Mont Blanc, on the far side of a grassy shoulder,
we walked right through. *Don't be afraid,*
they're only cows. — I'm telling you,
over there, no, on the right, there's one
with balls, where . . . — Speed up,
she's right behind us! And in the evening,
her panties were tangled with the devil's in
laughter and the smells of straw, life
danced like a vertigo of stars but
only water never forgets its course,
and in the city, after midday, there are
no more cows: she goes by
slowly, that lady, at a distance of years,
without recognizing, and passes by! While there's
honking at l'Opéra because a bus driver
is weeping in the gutter; you're left to quibble
about memories like some excommunicate, plunge
your nose in your *Spaten,* then
write this right away, what's left of it
is more fragile than a spider's house,
but you must feel as if any passerby
could get your table hurled at his jaw.

Halte en montagne

Une femme caresse ses jambes,
Les étire après trois heures passées
Au brûloir de la paroi. Tout ce qui remplit
Le temps prend soudain de la durée
Quand l'oxygène comble sa dette
En soulevant les seins ; l'ombre fraîche
Fait échanger quelques mots
Sur une recette de viande au citron —
Mais quel vin ? Tu sais que le citron
Est impitoyable, dit-elle, face au couloir
De granit, alors que dans sa prunelle
Aux reflets pâles éclate la tache
Jaune d'un parapente qui embarque
La montagne entière dans un sifflement.

A Pause in the Mountains

A woman massages her legs
And stretches them after three hours spent
On the grill of the rock face. Everything which fills
Time up suddenly seems to last
When oxygen makes good on its debt
By lifting up her breasts; the cool shade
Leads to a casual exchange of words
About a recipe, a roast cooked with lemon.
But what wine to serve? You know how unforgiving
Lemon is, she says, facing the granite
Gully, while into her irises'
Pale gleaming bursts the yellow stain
Of a glider which carries off
The whole mountain with its whistling.

La cascade

L'atrabilaire relâche sa lecture
Pour contempler une cascade creusant
Son chemin vers le fond simple
Du monde. Elle baigne au passage
Les seins d'une femme, et les aréoles
Arrachent encore quelques battements
Aux veines des promeneurs discrets
Qui rôdent aux confins du silence
Et de l'herbe. *On ne devient pas meilleur*
Mais seulement plus rusé, dit-on
Dans le journal, tandis que des gouttes
D'eau fraîche viennent faire un bruit
Pur au bas de la feuille où se déploie
La nécrologie d'un grand écrivain.

The Waterfall

The grouch abstracts himself from what he's reading
To contemplate a waterfall that hollows
Its way toward the world's
Simple depths. As it passes, it bathes
A woman's breasts, and the areolas
Provoke a few pulsations in the veins
Of discreet hikers who prowl around
The borders of that silence
And that grass. *One doesn't become better,*
Merely cleverer, it says in
The newspaper, while a few drops
Of cool water come to make a pure
Noise at the bottom of a page on which is laid out
A major writer's obituary.

La fête

On revenait du bois de pins
En saluant au passage le cuisinier
Tôt retraité : sa fille était morte
A moto et il élevait des chiens
De race *airedale,* affectueux et roux.
Quelques jardins plus loin, c'était
L'heure du café accompagné de sablés
Dans un salon où les portraits
Rappelaient Stalingrad puis les Aurès.
La voix de la dame disait n'avoir jamais
Aimé la guerre ni ceux qui l'obligaient,
Encore enfant, à manger sous la table.
Sur la faïence des grandes tasses,
Un couple marchait vers une fête foraine.

The Fair

Coming back from the pine woods, we greeted
The cook who retired early: his daughter died
In a motorcycle crash; now he raised dogs,
Airedales, reddish and affectionate.
A few gardens farther on, it was
Time for coffee and shortbread cookies
In a living room where portraits brought back
Stalingrad, then the Aurès mountains.
The woman's voice declared she had never
Liked wars or the people who made her eat
Under the table when she was still a child.
On the ceramic of the coffee cups
A couple ambled toward a county fair.

Dinard

On marche ensemble sur le promenoir
Au pied des maisons d'anglais
Fin dix-neuvième. Les mimosas résistent
Au vent de la Manche qui jette
Une lumière cadmium à fond violet
Sur les grosses marches de pierre
Où tourne une silhouette de femme
Perdue dans son manteau : écume,
Où bat parfois comme un cœur
Invisible le temps jamais rattrapé
Des images, quand la pensée
Pleure de rage devant le bel
Ordre elliptique du jour d'ardoise
Que tend la corde d'un cerf-volant.

Dinard

We walk together on the promenade
Below houses where the English lived
A hundred years ago. Mimosas hold
Out against the Channel wind which throws
A purple-grounded cadmium light
On the stout stone steps
Where a woman's shape revolves,
Lost in her coat: foam, in which
There sometimes beats like an invisible
Heart the unrecaptured time
Of images, when thought
Weeps with rage before the beautiful
Ellipsis of a slate-gray day
Held aloft on a kite string.

Au restaurant

Le patron fait des omelettes aux cèpes,
De la tarte flambée et la pâte
Même des choux pour les profiteroles.
Au mur sont encadrés des journaux
D'avant-guerre où Saint-Exupéry
Raconte Madrid et les fusils pour deux.
Coffres et cuivres sont astiqués
Pour survivre à tous les départs,
Le courant d'air malmène un client
Qui s'est trompé de pull-over
Et sa compagne aux mains lentes regarde
Sur les eaux de l'Atlantique décoller
Un immense hydravion : sa version
Luxe comptait des chambres à coucher.

At the Restaurant

The owner-chef makes wild-mushroom omelettes,
Flamed desserts, and even his own dough
For profiterole puffs.
On the wall are framed newspapers
From before the war where Saint-Exupéry
Tells about Madrid, one rifle for two men.
Metal chests and copper bowls are polished
To survive all departures.
The draft manhandles a client
Who has worn the wrong sweater,
As his companion with the careful hands
Watches the Atlantic takeoff
Of a huge hydroplane: the luxury
Version even had bedrooms.

La vieille compagne

Il veut se faire
Opérer mais
Il est fou
Les médecins sont
Fous, et puis
La voix
Au ciel elle lui a dit
Jamais !
Il faut de simples
Cataplasmes
De concombre
Beaucoup d'amour
D'ailleurs s'il meurt
Elle se tuera.

The Old Wife

He wants to have
The operation but
He's crazy
The doctors are
Crazy and then
Raising her voice to
The heavens she told him
Never!
He just needs simple
Cucumber compresses
A lot of love
Anyway if he dies
She'll kill herself.

Les camarades

Ils ont méprisé
Le bonheur
Et n'obéissaient
Qu'à eux-mêmes,
N'acceptant pas
Que leurs compagnes
Fussent heureuses.
Ils pouvaient
Les sodomiser, mais
Leur interdisaient
Tout sentiment.
Ils vieillissent
Avec des femmes
Devenues méchantes.

The Comrades

They disdained
Happiness
And would obey only
Themselves,
Could not permit
Their spouses
To be happy.
They might
Sodomize them but
Forbade them
Any feelings.
They grew old
With women
Who had turned spiteful.

Stratford

L'une avait des cheveux blonds
Et ne les penchait guère
Que sur les redoutables héros de ses livres,
Quand ils se battent pour une captive
Aux jambes encore entravées ; l'autre
Portait un corsage couleur de lièvre
Sans rien d'éperdu dans sa forme
Et s'essayait au tremblé de la voix
Pour faire vrai quand elle disait qu'aucun air
N'innocente un monde à faux proverbes
Et meurtres cachés. Elles avaient appris
A se connaître en aimant Hamlet
Et les hommes hésitants, à Stratford,
Comme il convient. Dans la fumée,
Les cris du *pub,* l'acteur démaquillé
Avait aussi lampé des bières sans fin,
Tandis qu'Ophélie riait chaque nuit
De plus en plus haut, en gagnant
Contre de vrais gaillards
Des parties de fléchettes rouge et or.
Les gens parfois chantaient *O mistress mine.*
Et certains finissaient par se prendre la main.
Il y eut même un soir une vraie foudre : Edmund,
Bâtard de *Lear,* et le silence chargé d'armes
Soudain, de craquements de planches,
De mots obscènes contre les héritiers : *Toi,*
Nature, O ma déesse... Elles rentraient tard,

Stratford

One of them had blond hair
And only let it down
Over the formidable heroes of her books
When they fought over a captive
Whose legs were still bound; the other
Wore a mouse-colored blouse
With nothing distraught about her bearing
And made her voice waver
To sound right when she declared that no song
Absolved a world full of false proverbs
And hidden murders. They got to know
Each other because they both loved Hamlet
And hesitant men, in Stratford,
Appropriately. In the smoke
And noise of the pub, the actor scrubbed of makeup
Had also guzzled endless beers,
While Ophelia laughed louder every night,
As she defeated some strapping locals
At matches of red-and-gold-tipped darts.
Sometimes people sang "O Mistress Mine."
And a few of them finally took each other's hands.
There was even a real thunderbolt one night: Edmund,
The bastard in *Lear*, and the silence loud with weapons,
Suddenly, the creaking of the boards,
Obscene oaths against the heirs: *Thou,*
Nature, art my Goddess . . . They left late

Sous un vertige d'étoiles, festin de rythmes
Filant par-delà les questions vers l'ombre bleue,
Buissons, flocons et lèvres de la rivière,
Cherchant l'issue, cherchant les impensables
Fleurs lucides, et s'arrêtant ensemble
Au rebord de jardins ensauvagés pour mieux
S'imaginer chaque syllabe sans cesse
A bout de branche, à bout d'idée
Nouvelle et de dépense avide : comment
Echapper au legs, comment devenir
Quelqu'un d'autre, à sa juste distance,
Et moyen pour les yeux de ne jamais
Durcir ce qu'ils regardent, même quand
La vie va prendre cette forme unique :
A l'avenir présentez-vous dans les délais.
Quelque chose était là malgré tout dans les haies
Parmi les liserons; il faudrait vingt ans
D'oubli pour en retrouver la douceur.

Beneath a vertigo of stars, a feast of meter
Spinning their questions out toward the blue shadow,
Bushes, flakes, and lips of the stream,
Looking for the exit, looking for the unthinkable
Conscious flowers, and stopping together
At the edge of the overgrown gardens in order
To better imagine each syllable always
At the tip of a branch, at the tip of a new
And avidly spent idea: how to
Escape a legacy, how to become
Someone different, at the right distance,
And a way for one's eyes never to
Harden what they look at, even when
Life would consist of that single directive:
In future you will report at the assigned time.
Something was there after all in the hedges
Among the convolvuli, it would take twenty years
Of forgetting to reclaim its sweetness.

Le salon de musique

Pour le plancher, c'est un point
De Hongrie : chaque carré fait de quatre
Carrés dont les lattes semblent
Se poursuivre, et les murs sont plaqués
De cuir et d'acajou. D'ici on surveillait
L'usine, on servait les éclairs, on jouait
Beethoven en rabotant les ironies,
Et quand tout a fermé on a mis pour
Trente ans les gendarmes. Il ne vient
Plus personne, le *Pleyel* est foutu
Et le docteur ajoute qu'un bon coup
De chaleur c'est quatorze de ses vieux
En moins dans le bourg, à quinze cents
Francs chacun par an, on fait vite le calcul.

The Music Room

As for the parquet, it's in a fishbone pattern:
Each square made of four other
Squares whose planks seem to pursue
Each other, and the walls are covered with
Mahogany and leather. From here, they watched
The factory, they were served éclairs, they played
Beethoven, planing down his ironies,
And when it was all closed up police were posted
Here for thirty years. No one comes any more,
The Pleyel is shot to hell
And the doctor adds that with one good heat
Wave, there'll be fourteen less of his
Old geezers in town, at fifteen hundred
Francs apiece a year, you can add that up fast enough.

La leçon de chant

Nous sommes en mai, c'est toute la nature
Qui tape, débrouillez-vous, entrez
En bousculant comme une épée, et que
Ça suive, mettez donc des fantasmes
Mais debout sur les consonnes, avec
Le souffle, sinon quand on redescend
C'est l'estomac qui sort, et pas besoin
De vous asseoir sur votre *la,* amenez-le
Devant, tournez toujours dans la couleur
Et sans coquetterie : vous êtes payée
Pour un programme, d'ailleurs ce soir
Vous enlevez cette mâchoire, la force
Du suraigu est ici, dit-elle, en faisant
Un geste léger, des tempes vers le front.

The Singing Lesson

It's the month of May, all nature
Is knocking, collect yourself, make your entrance
Rush in like a sword, and let
The rest follow, get some fantasy into it
But stand up to the consonants, with
Your breath, otherwise, on the low notes
You'll look pot-bellied, and no need
To sit on your *la*, bring it forward, always turn
Toward the color, don't flirt: you're being paid
For a concert, and by the way, this evening
Tuck in that jaw, all the strength
Of the high notes is here, she says, making
A swift movement, from temples to forehead.

La belle

Surgit soudain la dissonance
En *si majeur,* brutale comme
Un coup d'œil d'hypocrite qui a
Surpris l'intérieur du genou
D'une femme et ne sait plus
Que faire de sa rage. Elle traverse
La pièce et revient en violence
De poing sur le clavier : *joue donc*
La fausse erreur, rétorquent
Les sons rieurs qui vont quand même
Au vent avec les cris, le grand
Soleil et les ballons d'enfants,
Car la belle, tu le sais, ça n'est
Jamais qu'un des temps de la bête.

Beauty

A dissonance wells up suddenly
In E major, brutal as
A hypocrite's glance which has
Taken the underside of a woman's
Knee by surprise and no longer knows
What to do with this rage that crosses
The room and returns with the violence
Of a fist on the keyboard. *Now play*
The wrong false note, snap back
The laughing sounds speeding toward
The courtyard with the shouts, the bright
Sunlight, and the children's rubber balls.
Their beauty, you know, is always merely
One of the tempi of the beast.

Variations

Elle sait aussi qu'il avait dit : *Les autres*
chient du marbre, et qu'il jouait
parfois en plein, disons, bordel (c'est
dans *Amadeus*), ça donne, *Ah ! vous dirai-je,*
du goût à la douceur des notes, entre marches
et feintes, où le temps ne fait pas de cadeau :
elle joue, *ré, mi, do, tou-our-ment,* un *mi*
d'un quart de temps dans un grand mot,
pour dire le bon faux pas, et le silence
n'est pas une forme qui s'éloigne : c'est pour
tout rassembler quand le traversent les fulgurantes
exactitudes, l'arpège de l'autre main. Plus tard,
la roue du cœur, l'ivresse, les mots fêlés,
ou tenir les étoiles ! Ce soir *Ah ! vous dirai-je,*
ce n'est que le début de la course et déjà
le reflet ironique de soi, tandis que l'utopie
discrètement se tient derrière la lampe dans
les mains de maman, ce soir, le temps est un octave.

Variations

She already knows that he had said, *The rest of them*
shit marble, and that he sometimes played
in, shall we say, disorderly houses (it's
in *Amadeus*), which produced *Ah, vous dirais-je,*
a taste with the notes' sweetness, between the black
and white keys, where time gives nothing away:
she plays, *re mi do tou-our-ment,* a *mi*
that's a quarter-note in a big word,
to utter the right misstep, and silence
is not a figure walking away: it's there to
bring everything together when it's crossed
by fiery certainties, the other hand's arpeggios. Later
the heart's wheeling, drunkenness, shattered words,
or holding on to stars. Tonight *Ah, vous dirais-je*
is only the start of the race, and already
the ironic reflection of herself, while utopia
stays discreetly behind the lamp in
mama's hands, tonight, time is an octave.

acknowledgments

Translations appeared previously in the following:

"The Answer": *The Paris Review*
"The Anthropophage Victim": *Lyric*
"Arènes de Lutèce": *Modern Poetry in Translation* (U.K.)
"Bacchus": *Ambit* (U.K.)
"The Bus Driver": *Prairie Schooner; PN Review* (U.K.)
"The Doctor": *The Kenyon Review*
"The Double": *New Letters*
"The End of the Wine Harvest": *Columbia*
"The Fair": *PN Review* (U.K.)
"The Flock": *Two Lines; Rattapallax; Ambit* (U.K.)
"The Frisbee": *Ambit* (U.K.)
"Goddess of Spring ": *Circumference*
"Hail to the Artist": *Ploughshares; Poetry London* (U.K.)
"Homilies": *Rattapallax*
"Insect": *New Letters*
"Jardin du Luxembourg: Bright Interval": *PN Review* (U.K)
"Jean-Paul de Dadelsen": *Poetry*
"Knothead": *Agni*
"The Little Disgraces": *PN Review* (U.K.)
"The Mill": *Pleiades*
"The Music Room": *The Kenyon Review*
"The Nightmare": *Poetry*
"The Night Watchman": *Pleiades*
"No Rhymes": *Poetry International*

"The Old Wife": *Ploughshares*

"Parc de la Cité": *Lyric; Modern Poetry in Translation* (U.K.)

"A Pause in the Mountains": *PN Review* (U.K.)

"Place de la République": *The Denver Quarterly; The Times Literary Supplement* (U.K.)

"Poppies": *Columbia*

"Quai des Orfèvres": *The Times Literary Supplement* (U.K.)

"The Question": *Circumference*

"Rear Window": *Denver Quarterly; Poetry London* (U.K.)

"Recess": *Two Lines; Rattapallax*

"Rue de Tournon": *The Paris Review*

"The Sailboat Pond": *The New Yorker*

"The Scarab Bookshop": *Circumference; PN Review* (U.K.)

"September": *Rattapallax; PN Review* (U.K.)

"Serenade": *Prairie Schooner*

"Six-Thirty": *Poetry*

"The Spinners": *American Poetry Review*

"Spiritual Distress": *Poetry International; PN Review* (U.K.)

"The Supermarket": *Poetry International*

"Tigers' Gold": *Modern Poetry in Translation* (U.K.)

"Treason": *American Poetry Review; Ambit* (U.K.)

"Truth": *The Kenyon Review; PN Review* (U.K.)

"Variations": *Verse*

"Verlaine": *Poetry*

"The Warm Shadow": *The Antioch Review*

"The Waterfall": *The Kenyon Review; PN Review* (U.K.)

"Spiritual Distress" and "Treason" appeared in *New European Poets*, ed. Kevin Prufer and Wayne Miller (St. Paul: Graywolf, 2008).

"The Bus Driver" and "Variations" appeared in *The Yale Anthology of Twentieth-Century French Poetry,* ed. Mary Ann Caws (New Haven: Yale University Press, 2004).

"Verlaine" and "Rue de Tournon" appeared in *Twentieth-Century French Poems,* ed. Stephen Romer (London: Faber and Faber, 2002).

Hédi Kaddour's poems were originally published in the following collections:

La fin des vendanges (Paris: Editions Gallimard, 1989)
"Acquis"
"Les coquelicots"
"La détresse spirituelle"
"Le double"
"La fin des vendanges"
"Noces du chacal"
"L'or des tigres"
"Pas de rimes"
"Les petites infamies"
"La pocharde"
"Récréation"
"Septembre"
"Trahison"
"Variations"

Jamais une ombre simple (Paris: Editions Gallimard, 1994)
"A Jean Follain"
"Arbres"

"Le cauchemar"

"Le chauffeur"

"La communion" ("Les chiens")

"La demande"

"Fruits sur la fenêtre"

"La gardeuse d'oies"

"Jean-Paul de Dadelsen"

"Loin de Byzance: L'âme de victime"

"Le mètre et le chagrin"

"Le moulin"

"La pièce d'or"

"Salut l'artiste"

"Le serpent"

"Stratford"

"Supermarché"

"Le troupeau"

Passage au Luxembourg (Paris: Editions Gallimard, 2000)

"Arènes de Lutèce"

"Au restaurant"

"Bacchus"

"Le bassin"

"La belle"

"La calomnie d'après Apelle"

"Les camarades"

"La cascade"

"La chiffonnerie"

"Cybèle"

"Déesse du Printemps"

"Dinard"
"Dix-huit heures trente"
"Le docteur"
"Eclaircie"
"Evolène"
"Fenêtre sur cour"
"La fête"
"Les fileuses"
"Le *Frisbee*"
"Halte en montagne"
"Insecte"
"La leçon de chant"
"La librairie du Scarabée"
"La meule"
"L'ombre
"L'ombre tiède"
"Parc de la Cité"
"La petite troupe"
"Les pommettes"
"Quai des Orfèvres"
"La réponse"
"La République"
"Rue de Tournon"
"Le salon de musique"
"Sérénade"
"La tentation derrière l'église"
"Tête de nœud"
"Le veilleur"
"La vérité"

"Verlaine"
"La victime anthropophage"
"La vieille compagne"
"Le vin nouveau"